THE CLOSING HEADLINES
Inside Scottish Broadcasting

By the same author:

Travels in a Small Country
Conversations in a Small Country

The Closing Headlines
Inside Scottish Broadcasting

by
Kenneth Roy

CARRICK MEDIA
Irvine

Copyright Kenneth Roy

All rights reserved

First published in 1993 by
Carrick Media
2/7 Galt House
31 Bank Street
Irvine KA12 0LL

Typeset by Saxon Printing, Derby
Printed in Great Britain by Bookcraft, Midsomer Norton, Avon

British Library Cataloguing-in-Publication Data
A catalogue record for this book is available from the British Library

ISBN 0 946724 32 6

Contents

1	Nothing doing	11
2	A suit and a haircut	18
3	"It's Scotland's oil"	26
4	Wizard prang	36
5	Children of the Pissed	43
6	Dirty tricks	51
7	Sort of famous	58
8	Canteen characters	66
9	Mods and blondes	74
10	Department of miracles	82
11	David Niven changes his shirt	91
12	Limbo	99
13	How to refuse £50,000	109
14	The prize	118
15	A clean sheet of paper	126
16	Why does my Pekinese keep fainting?	135
17	Sandy's Indian summer	145
18	"You'll end up lonely"	153
19	Sort of anonymous	162
20	Small country	168
21	Epilogue	177
	Index	*182*

Acknowledgements

I wish to thank Chatto & Windus for permission to quote from Norman MacCaig's poem, London to Edinburgh, which is included in his Collected Poems (new edition, 1990), and George Outram & Company for permission to quote at length an article by Gordon Petrie which appeared in the now-defunct Sunday Standard in October 1981.

It is made clear in the text where I use brief extracts from: The Biggest Aspidistra in the World, by Peter Black (BBC Books); Headlines: the media in Scotland, edited by David Hutchison (EUSPB); and Inside BBC Scotland 1975-80: a personal view, by Alastair Hetherington (Whitewater Press).

I am grateful to my wife, Margaret, who read the text in draft and made helpful suggestions; to my colleague, Fiona MacDonald, for all her assistance in bringing the book to press; and to my cat Tabitha, who kept me company while I wrote it. She was asleep most of the time; I hope that the book does not have the same soporific effect on others.

Preface

I have not dedicated this book to anyone in particular, although three people kept coming to mind during the writing: Sandy Webster, one of the great characters of Scottish journalism; Jameson Clark, for his warmth and conviviality; and Donald N. Macdonald, perhaps my closest colleague in broadcasting, who died just as I reached his chapter. Indeed I realised before I finished that most of the people I have liked best in my working life are dead and that I miss them badly.

These, then, are the closing headlines in more senses than one. Part of the book is about friends who have gone; what is left is an attempt to come to terms with a career in broadcasting which began in 1972 and continued, with some interruptions, until its farcical conclusion in the autumn of 1992. This was a period of great change and some hope not only in Scottish broadcasting but in Scotland itself. Both are duller now; I think I got the best of it.

K.R.
Irvine
August 31 1993

1

Nothing doing

Ernest Purdy of the Glasgow Herald looked wrongly cast for the raffish part of crime reporter. He was a mild man with a neat moustache and a house in the suburbs. Yet his working life was bizarre: he started work when most of his colleagues were thinking about the pub, crashed into bed at dawn, and maintained this nocturnal existence for the better part of his career.

Although it would have suited few journalists, the graveyard shift seemed to suit Ernest. The job involved an endless trawl of Glasgow police stations, one after the other in rotation throughout the night. "Anything doing?" he would ask cheerfully. "Quiet night, Ernie," they would lie, and on he would move to the next.

The other reporters prayed that Ernest should be preserved for the nation as paddle steamers and ancient monuments are preserved. None of us fancied his disagreeable beat, particularly as there was so little copy in it (the Herald was not much interested in crime) and so little opportunity to shine. But when Ernest took a night off, or went on one of his caravan holidays, we were expected to cover. The entry "7.30pm to 3.30am" in John Ritchie's newsroom diary was the most dreaded of short straws. I drew it regularly.

The crime reporter travelled in some style in a stately office car with a driver, Bob, who said that I reminded him of Jimmy Maxton, the Clydeside revolutionary. At the age of 20 I preferred girls to revolution, night life to night shifts, sex to violence. However, there were times when even a razor-slashing would have been a welcome distraction from the monotony of the job. The only violence I saw was up against a wall in Govan police station, when one policeman held a prisoner while another kicked and punched him.

"Anything doing?"

"Naw, son, nothin'."

After the last call of the night, I sprinted from the staff door in Mitchell Lane to Central Station for the milk train to Larbert, walked three miles home, and snatched a few hours' sleep before the 2 to 10 shift. After a year of this punishing routine, I went down with a bad bout of glandular fever and was off work for six weeks. I still felt unwell when I returned to the office. I knew I must escape the drudgery of the Glasgow Herald's anti-social hours, but was far from clear what to do next. So I tried a desperate remedy. I decided to ask Sandy Webster for a job.

Webster, an irascible tabloid hack, edited the muck-raking Sunday Mail, an unlikely spiritual home for a delicate young refugee from the Glasgow Herald who was liable to be shocked by the police's more robust interrogation techniques. But, like thousands of other punters in years to come, I dialled Webster.

"Who is it?" demanded a gruff voice.

"Roy. Kenneth Roy."

"And who the hell is Kenneth Roy?"

"Kenneth Roy of the Herald. The Glasgow Herald."

"Never heard of you. What do you want?"

"I thought you might have a job for me."

"What sort of a job?"

"As a reporter. I've done some pieces you might have noticed."

"No jobs here for you," he growled. And, then, in utter exasperation: "Oh, all right, I'll see you for 10 minutes. But can't promise you a thing. Tomorrow. Three o'clock. Goodbye."

Like a coward, I stood him up.

A more inviting possibility of escape came in the form of a late-night telephone call from a stranger with a familiar name and a soft Hebridean accent. Finlay J. Macdonald of the BBC said that he was an admirer of my journalism and wondered if I would like to work with him on a TV documentary.

I trusted BBC producers almost as much as I trusted Govan policemen. Five years earlier the ambitious young theatre critic of the Falkirk Mail had written to BBC Scotland with a proposition for improving the radio coverage of amateur drama, only to have his idea woundingly rejected by a producer who pointed out that at the same age he had been writing about amateur drama for a rather more important newspaper. I showed W. Gordon Smith's letter to no one, but kept it as a warning never to get ideas above my radio station.

Nor could I be sure of Finlay J. Macdonald, who was slurring his words and might – it momentarily occurred to me – have phoned the wrong man. But better Finlay J. drunk than Govan police station sober. In a corner of the newsroom, Ernest Purdy was studying back numbers of Camping and Caravanning, always an ominous signal that the Larbert milk train would not be long delayed. *Of course* I would like to work on a TV documentary.

With a dispiriting sigh Finlay said that the BBC wished him to make a documentary about the problems of old people. Deadly dull, he knew, but perhaps there was a way of humanising the subject. Any ideas? Next morning I called him with a suggestion that we should build the programme around an old woman living alone in my home village of Bonnybridge, Stirlingshire.

"Bonnybridge," he repeated in his mellifluous brogue, as if I had just recommended a trip to Jupiter. "I'm not sure I've ever been in Bonnybridge. Where is it, exactly?"

I explained that it was an industrial village near Falkirk, notable for its brickworks where avenging fathers threatened to send their sons if they didn't stick in at school. I might have impressed him by adding that Bonnybridge, improbably, had been a temporary hiding place of the Stone of Destiny after its removal from Westminster Abbey – buried by John Rollo, a local industrialist and patriot, under the floor of my uncle George Bernard's office.

Finlay said that he would visit the village to see for himself and meanwhile I should work on a treatment for the programme. I hadn't the faintest idea what he had in mind but made approving noises. We had never met, and his casual approach on the telephone bordered on the whimsical. Strange, too, that there was no mention of money. (Not so strange, when I got to know the BBC and its funny old ways.)

The sight of Bonnybridge must have dismayed Finlay, for when we next spoke, he sounded discouraged. He said tactfully that it was not the prettiest village he had ever seen. In my mind's eye I imagined him gazing incredulously at the broken-down bridge over the impossibly muddy burn, the old-fashioned flannels in the Co-op window, the seedy picture house, the Italian caff, the ugly

The Closing Headlines

RC church on the hill, the disintegrating public hall smelling of old wood where people called Rechabites met, the Junior Sec with its whiff of failure, the enormous local authority housing scheme of drab post-war uniformity. A poet either kind or blind had included Bonnybridge in a children's verse praising the virtues of Britain's most attractive villages, and in our primary classes we had recited it straight-faced for fear of the belt. Bonnybridge had few other recorded admirers, least of all the people of Falkirk who referred to it witheringly as "dirty Bonnybrig". Yes, one could see that Finlay must have been discouraged.

Yet there was also a note of resignation in his voice: although Bonnybridge had turned out to be an appalling mistake, he was going to make the best of it. Besides, he had met the old woman who was to become the subject of our film, 79-year-old Helen Smith, and liked her. Now events moved unexpectedly quickly. I wrote a commentary of sorts, but in the style of a rather ponderous Glasgow Herald article rather than a terse broadcast script. Finlay knocked it about with brutal professionalism. By the time The World of Mrs Smith reached the screen it retained one or two of my original phrases but was largely unrecognisable from the inadequate draft.

His secretary sent me a copy of the production schedule. The crew would assemble in the Royal, a hotel almost as deceptively named as Bonnybridge itself. I couldn't see what my presence would add to the occasion and stayed at home. Finlay rang. "We're here," he said testily, "and wondering if you're ever going to join us."

When I arrived they were drinking coffee in a gloomy anteroom. Finlay, with his kind face and gentle smile, had the demeanour of a troubled soul who was bravely enduring life's many disappointments, of which Bonnybridge and Kenneth Roy were the latest. He eyed his colleagues with amused detachment, his voice seldom rising above a whisper. All this I found unsettling.

The "workers" (to stretch a point) were three or four men each more carelessly dressed than the next, whose silences were punctuated by laconic jokes and cynical laughter. A mood of deep apathy pervaded the room and I doubted whether anything short of an A-bomb approaching from Polmont would have shifted it. But

The Closing Headlines

I learned a few years later that there had been nothing unusual about the scene in the Royal Hotel: TV technicians always start the day looking as if there has been a death in the family.

Between shifts I followed the crew around, contributing little and feeling surplus to requirements. Mrs Smith coped stoically with celebrity status and the imposition of BBC personnel camped day after day in her tiny living room. She was filmed taking in the milk, shopping, reading the paper, reminiscing about her dead husband, going to an old folk's social, chatting with friends, watching the telly, locking up at night, each mundane ritual beautifully observed by Stuart Wyld's camera. Indeed The World of Mrs Smith with its concentration on microscopic detail and absence of formal interviews was an early example of the "fly on the wall" documentary technique which, in a harsher and more intrusive form, became fashionable a decade or so later.

I sensed that Finlay was unhappy. A Celtic gloom would descend which a visit to the bar of the Royal did not invariably lift. One evening, after a few drinks, he talked dismissively of our programme, hinting that it was something to be got out of the way before a more significant project came along. Did I know, he demanded, that he was the first radio producer in Britain to have brought a Graham Greene novel to the air? I didn't. However, like most people, I had admired A Boy from Harris, his documentary about the Hebrides. Compared with such a fine achievement, a fortnight among the old age pensioners of dirty Bonnybrig must have seemed small beer. But the melancholy afflicting him could not be explained by professional dissatisfaction with one dull programme: the insecurities went deeper. (Later – many years later – he found professional fulfilment and personal happiness – but he found them away from the BBC.)

The World of Mrs Smith slipped on air with all the razzle of a well-kept secret. I was named as researcher in Radio Times though not in the programme credits, and received my first BBC contract followed by a small cheque. In the Scottish Daily Express, Don Whyte gave the programme a favourable review, praising its tact and sympathy and suggesting that it should be repeated. It never was.

The enigmatic figure of Finlay J. disappeared from my life as abruptly as he had arrived. There were no more late-night telephone calls to the Glasgow Herald newsroom, no more lunchtime confessionals in the Royal Hotel, no more offers of socially-conscious documentaries. Some months later, a schools producer, Gordon Menzies, at Finlay's prompting, auditioned me in the Glasgow studios along with about two dozen others. I froze in front of the camera and told myself afterwards that I hadn't wanted the job anyway.

By this stage I was reporting the High Court. At the end of most trials, a desperate ritual unfolded. A trap-door opened in the dock, the prisoner was bundled into a steep stairwell – "Take him down" commanded the scarlet-robed judge – and a woman in the spectator's gallery screamed. Always the trap-door; always the scream. One became used to this harrowing scene, if not quite immune.

One of the few consolations of the job was the occasional exclusive inspired by Winifred Ewing's inside knowledge of the Glasgow legal fraternity. As secretary of the Glasgow Bar Association, Mrs Ewing rang fairly regularly and became my best contact; actually, my only one. Since the Herald had many columns of space for local news, her name was rarely out of the paper.

Then, without knowing it, I wrote an article which offended her. She went straight to the deputy editor, George MacDonald Fraser, a remote figure though not of the same Olympian detachment as the editor himself, the mysterious Alastair Warren. Fraser preferred the solitude of his Buchanan Street eyrie to mixing it in the newsroom. We were told that he was writing a novel and did not wish to be disturbed. All journalists were supposed to be writing novels, but unlike the rest of us Fraser did seem to be committing dialogue to paper. The sharp tongue of some local solicitor nagging him about one of his reporters must have been a nuisance.

When the portly executive emerged from a meeting with the lady, he was visibly shaken. I told Fraser that the paper had been generous to her and that I resented the complaint. "Just get the bloody woman off my back," he replied impatiently. Perhaps he was going through a bad patch with Flashman.

Not long afterwards, the deputy editor left the paper as journalists dream of quitting. Offered a spectacular advance for his novel, he was advised by a far-sighted accountant to seek tax exile in the Isle of Man. So he did. And the rich and famous author was never troubled again by the likes of Winifred Ewing.

I gave the secretary of the Glasgow Bar Association a wide berth, watched the trap-door open and shut for a few more months, then quit. Warren sent a farewell memo which ended bleakly: "You could have had a good career in journalism." A few weeks later I married Margaret, who had played my fiancée in an amateur production of Quiet Wedding, went to live by the sea at Portobello (some called it Joppa, which was considered posher), and started a new job turning out soul-destroying promotional guff about Scottish industry.

In November of that year – 1967 – I was startled to hear the sensational result of a parliamentary by-election in Hamilton. It couldn't be the same Winifred Ewing, could it? A national heroine, the papers were calling her. Well, well.

Mrs Ewing was appalled by the casual cruelties of the House of Commons, where she was roughly treated and dined alone under a portrait of Benjamin Disraeli. "Interruptions every time I spoke," she recalled bitterly when I interviewed her 20 years later. "Personal insults. Abuse. It's all there in Hansard. All recorded for posterity."

Like her, I hated my new job. It almost made me nostalgic for the Larbert milk train. I resigned as soon as possible, bought a printing press, and installed it in a Victorian villa on the edge of the Midlothian shale bings. For several years I led a precarious Bohemian existence with my young wife and two small sons. A bolshie magazine, though widely admired, was not a commercial success, and a touring theatre company failed to draw the crowds. I crawled out of bed one morning and counted unpaid bills for £3,000.

It was a perilous spot for a house of frail construction. Part of the roof blew off in one of the gales which gusted up from the abandoned oil village of Oakbank. Early one morning, as we lay in bed discussing our lack of prospects, the toast caught fire. A cat we had just inherited fled in disgust while the kitchen blazed.

"You could have had a good career in journalism." It sounded suspiciously like an epitaph. I was 25 years old.

2

A suit and a haircut

The correspondents of the Guardian and the Times, who worked out of the Glasgow Herald newsroom, were the Laurel and Hardy of Scottish journalism, Brown of the Guardian being as short and round as Cochrane of the Times was tall and slender. Brown, who insisted on addressing me as "Kenny", had a direct, voluble manner while Cochrane, the more subtle of this engaging pair, peppered his conversation with droll ironies.

When he left the Guardian, Brown recommended me to the paper's northern editor as a possible replacement. This thrilling prospect evaporated during the interview in a Glasgow trade union club, where a world-weary Harry Whewell – such a terrific name for a Guardian man – gave me a cursory once-over.

Now it was Hugh Cochrane who came to the rescue. Having worked for the BBC as a presenter of political programmes, he had just been appointed head of news, a job held for too long by a cantankerous cove called Jimmy Kemp. The new man had been widely welcomed: a distinguished journalist with his pedigree and on-screen experience would at last invigorate the lacklustre output. "I need a few reporters in this place," he said. "How about it?"

The offer could not have been more fortuitous. The magazine was failing, the theatre company had gone down with all stagehands. But twice before I had flopped in auditions for television – once for Gordon Menzies, later for Maurice Lindsay at Border TV – confirming the view of Alastair Ford, drama critic of the Greenock Telegraph, who had said of one of my stage performances that I might do well enough on radio. Perhaps, putting it tactfully, I was not very "visual". Yet I would have to try again; you might say that I owed it to my creditors.

I told Hugh that I was interested; when was he auditioning?

The Closing Headlines

"There's no need for any of that nonsense," he said briskly. "Come in and we'll talk about it."

There was precious little to talk about. A fortnight later I joined the BBC as a reporter on a short-term contract which might or might not be renewed after six months. In a curious way the insecurity of the deal appealed to me. I was broke and drifting, without career or motivation; six months would give me some breathing space. When the contract expired and Hugh, flicking ash off one of his immaculate suits, shook his head sadly and showed me the door, as I guessed he would, so what? At heart I was still a Sixties' hippy rebelling against conformity. I would take the BBC's money and run. I was sure of one thing: I wouldn't be with this lot any longer than necessary.

When the new boy presented himself in the newsroom of Broadcasting House, Glasgow, at 9.30 one autumn morning in 1972, the editorial "conference" – a desultory daily meeting of news executives – had already begun. The daily newspapers were spread out across a long desk at the head of the room, and a middle-aged man was stubbing his finger at some item and laughing in a way which somehow managed to be jolly and menacing at the same time.

As lesser functionaries discussed each item in a duplicated list of events – mostly press conferences or PR stunts thinly disguised as news – the man with the deceptively jolly laugh fell silent. Judging by the way his scrubbed features turned red, he took a poor view of the agenda. Surely, I judged, few of these abject non-events would ever see the lens of a BBC camera. A surprising number did, however, materialise in some form in that evening's Scottish news.

For me, the most interesting news of the day was the explosive personality of George Sinclair, he of the jolly laugh, whose outbursts my new colleagues related with some relish. Here, they assured me, was a man who had been known in hotter tempers to wrench the telephone from its socket and hurl it across the room.

Although the Gothic horror stories concerning the producer of Reporting Scotland contained a strong element of myth, what mattered was the potency of the myth; and George Sinclair played up to his image as Glasgow hard man, an honours graduate of the Scottish Daily Mail's notorious school. But the performance lacked conviction. George was a softy at heart, and every so often it showed.

I came to like and admire him. His occasional fits were over quickly, without recriminations or grudges, and there was a rough integrity about his dealings with people. But there was a contrary and more disturbing view. Some feared him.

Reporting Scotland's presenter, Douglas Kynoch, who offered to show me the premises, wore an air of chronic anxiety which hinted that he might be one of those who feared George. I was too shy to ask Douglas why he was at work before noon when the programme went out six hours later and he had little to do but powder his nose and rehearse a script which began to appear no earlier than 3.30. Sheer terror might have propelled him into the newsroom unnecessarily early – or the hope, usually forlorn, that he would be given a studio interview or a film report to relieve the monotony and make him feel wanted. He was an intelligent man and, though not a journalist, could have handled a certain type of journalistic assignment without difficulty. Non-journalists in a newsroom were, however, suspect. As a result, a silly and snobbish apartheid segregated "reporters" from mere "readers".

I remember nothing of the tour of inspection apart from a presentiment of doom. As we trudged along endless corridors of civil service anonymity, it occurred to me that a fragile personality could easily go mad in a building so drab and featureless. More than a few did. Someone said, probably in jest, that it had in some former incarnation been a hospital for the mentally deranged. How could you tell the difference? Certainly the building was miscast as a palace of entertainments.

Studio B, where Douglas Kynoch put on the party face, was as makeshift as a transit camp, devoid of personality, and oppressively hot. The set, which looked substantial enough to "viewers at home", was in reality of flimsy construction, no more secure than a reporter's standard contract. Even when the cast arrived – the floor manager, the cameraman who never spoke, the autocue girl, the little man who was paid to sit in a corner every evening and read the Evening Times – the studio failed to come alive as a stage would have come alive; the experience remained essentially a triumph of engineering over humanity. And in the centre of this enervating arena sat the hapless presenter.

The serious action took place, not on the studio floor, but upstairs in the production gallery where the principal contributors to the morning's editorial think-tank re-assembled each evening around 5.45 for "transmission".

All afternoon I had watched yellow-coloured scripts, neatly typed and treble-spaced, gathering on a newsroom table, and admired the sense of purpose with which George Sinclair arranged them into a running order, a well-balanced mix of film reports, studio interviews, and "straight reads" (short items voiced by the presenter without visual amplification). It all seemed so meticulously prepared that as the programme director, Malcolm Coupar, left for the gallery to supervise the smooth running of the operation, I wondered why he brought to mind the condemned man in a Hollywood gas chamber. I was to find out soon enough. For it was not in the painstaking assembly of the day's news that George Sinclair came into his own but in the production gallery – as the virtuoso conductor of a modern re-enactment of Bedlam.

Although George had been a television executive for several years, spiritually he had never left newspapers. In newspapers it was possible actually to hold a front page. Stories could be introduced and dropped, jigged and rejigged, until almost the last minute and occasionally beyond. Television, on the other hand, despite the spurious aura of urgency it affected, worked to a more ponderous schedule. It took an amazingly long time to process a news film, edit it into a comprehensible shape, script it and get it on air. This was an intense source of frustration to newsdesk people who had been reared in the instant rough and tumble of the press. Most conceded defeat; George never did. For him, each working day was another round in the war against the lumbering technology of the medium.

So there was a remarkable contradiction between the two faces of Reporting Scotland – the solid, dependable programme which the viewers saw and the manic, impromptu creativity which brought it to the nation's teatable. George's bravura performance, if only the BBC had opened it to the paying public, might have been one of Scotland's more diverting tourist attractions.

His brilliant gift for "busking it" was needlessly complicated by the management's insistence on linking the programme from three studios only one of which (Glasgow) could offer colour. The scripts were shared among Kynoch and his monochrome partners, Renton Laidlaw in Edinburgh and Donny B. MacLeod in Aberdeen. Regional pride was satisfied, but technically the split operation made the 6 o'clock minefield more difficult to negotiate without a hitch. George, I think, loathed it.

Yet it was remarkable how seldom anything went visibly wrong. There was nothing to compare with the famous incident some years before, when the teatime slot was occupied by a light magazine rather than a news programme. The set simulated a book-lined study in which – this being a superior light magazine – the books were the real things and not the hollow cardboard versions favoured by the keepers of the tackier country house hotels. One night all the machines went down and the Scottish actor who was presenting the show was left stranded with several minutes to fill. Now, what would you have done? I will tell you what this man did. With magnificent presence of mind he strolled over to the bookshelf, picked out a volume at random, and read from it until it was time for the next programme.

George Sinclair would not have approved of a book-lined study as a set for Reporting Scotland. But there were occasions when his embattled newsreaders, struggling to maintain an outward show of coherence, would have welcomed a book or two as prop and standby – if not, indeed, a whole floor of the Mitchell Library.

On the second day they told me to prepare a short report of about 50 seconds (150 words at the normal broadcast rate of three per second), which I would deliver live in the studio. I have no recollection of the story or of how I performed, but I do remember feeling oddly nerveless about the whole experience. I had read somewhere that, in order to preserve your sanity, it was essential to forget that you were addressing half the nation and visualise instead a person sitting alone in a living room or watching with half an eye from the kitchen. This I discovered was excellent advice and surprisingly practical. It is, of course, how most people do watch television – not in large groups but on their own or with one or two others. Television has the further advantage that the mass audience, or series of tiny audiences, is electronically remote, unable to throw rotten tomatoes at the performer, and not really concentrating anyway.

(That paragraph was 163 words long – the equivalent of rather more than 50 broadcast seconds.)

Afterwards, George smiled encouragingly but said nothing – a form of high praise from him. Hugh Cochrane was less impressed. He quarrelled over my use of the phrase "a definite possibility" and asked teasingly how something that was only a possibility could be called definite. Here we enter a pedant's paradise. Tomorrow, if the weather is fine, I may take a boat to Arran and climb Goat Fell. That is so slim a possibility that it can be discounted. Alternatively, if the weather is poor, I may go home and continue writing this book. Now that is a possibility worthy of the name. A definite maybe, as they say in America. Yet I had to acknowledge that the scholarly man was, strictly speaking, correct: possibilities by definition cannot be definite.

His next complaint was more worrying than any solecism.

"I hope," he said lightly, "that you'll be getting yourself a suit and a haircut."

By orthodox BBC Scotland standards I was certainly unusual. I wore shoulder-length hair and, as well as a serviceable jacket, a nice shirt and a colourful tie, sported a pair of jeans which would not have permitted me access to the cocktail lounges and restaurants of Gleneagles Hotel after 7pm. But there was an important difference: television viewers, unlike waiters, could not actually see my jeans. So far as my mother-in-law in Gourock was concerned – for Mrs Campbell was my selected audience of one – I might have been wearing anything from the waist down.

Yet I could hardly tell Hugh, who had rescued me from penury or – horror! – the trap-door to some debtor's jail, that I disliked suits and preferred tweed jackets and denims. Some compromise would have to be reached. I decided that, for the next few months until I was fired, I would keep my hair at the BBC's prescribed length and buy a few pairs of "proper" trousers for the studio, while stopping short of the ultimate indignity. I got away with this strategy. I never did buy a suit.

Hugh, surprisingly to me, was rarely seen in the newsroom where his journalistic talents should have been employed but seemed to spend most of the day at "meetings" – the curse of the BBC's monstrous bureaucracy as I had not yet discovered. And when he was not at "meetings" he was in his room preparing "memos" or "papers" and generally acting the part of a head of department. A man of his creative instincts and acute perceptions must have found it difficult to adjust to the administrative function. And I suspected that he was unhappy with some of the journalists he had inherited.

In a very low mood, he called the troops into his room and delivered the works – all his pent-up frustrations released at last. The programme was not up to scratch. Scripts were shoddily written. Whole areas of Scottish life – politics he mentioned specifically, though he could have added the arts – were poorly covered. In short, the output stank. And this was no definite possibility. This, Hugh made clear, was a racing certainty.

The lecture was received in complete silence. Even though most of what he said was true or partly true, there wasn't much that any of us could have done about it; if the situation was so hopeless, logic dictated that he should comprehensively fire and re-hire. Eventually Campbell Barclay spoke up. He admitted that our reporting of Scottish politics left much to be desired. As the man responsible, he felt he should say that. But, he added, it was impossible for one reporter to cover industry and politics adequately, as he was expected to do. In the poisonous atmosphere, this reasonable point went unanswered.

Whatever Hugh's motive in calling it, the meeting achieved nothing. Lacking support from above or below, and in the absence of kindred spirits, he was left a sadder and more isolated figure. I saw less and less of him. One day I came back from a film assignment and was told that our head of news had resigned suddenly and was already out of the building. This news, though shocking and sad, was not entirely surprising. Hugh rebuilt a highly successful career in print journalism with the Glasgow Herald.

He was replaced by Ross Anderson, a Kirk elder, who was fond of a girn but kept his head down and avoided confrontation. Now that Hugh was gone, I felt exposed – I had turned out to be one of the few acquisitions of his short rule. But the new regime was amiable: I was still allowed to talk to my mother-in-law most nights.

Then I got a break. Renton Laidlaw, the Douglas Kynoch of Edinburgh, though the resemblance should not be pushed too far, had landed a job as a globe-trotting golf reporter/commentator and would soon be employing the peculiar vocabulary of that trade ("He'll not be happy with that one"; "I wonder what he's thinking in Spanish" etc). This left a vacancy in the capital city which, when offered, I seized for domestic as well as career reasons.

Unlike the peripatetic Laidlaw, I trotted each evening no further than the stopping train from Glasgow Central to Mid-Calder via Cambuslang, Uddingston, Shotts, Addiewell, and nine other stops along that melancholy route through the Lanarkshire blackbelt. By the time the programme finished, George Sinclair held his agonising post-mortem, and the two-hour journey home was over, my two children were in bed. Working in Edinburgh, the unfamiliar figure on the screen would no longer have to be pointed out as the man who once claimed to be their daddy. I might even be home for tea.

Professionally too it seemed the right move. I would be nearer the centre of Scotland's exciting future – a future which, like the big picture, was said to be coming soon. And I decided that, when it came, I wanted to be a part of it.

3
"It's Scotland's oil"

Let us, as disc jockeys say, go back in time – but only a bit – to the cat-disappearing, kitchen-blazing, roof-collapsing period before I became a television face. Few offered work, but one of those who did was Ian Jack, the gentle Indiaphile from North Queensferry, who had once accompanied me on a fact-finding tour of Blackhill, Glasgow's most notorious suburb. The result was a vivid piece of actuality reporting and caused something of a stir with its exposure of social conditions in parts which the Glasgow Herald did not normally reach. When I re-read the piece years later I was embarrassed by its sub-Hemingway prose and tore it up in a fit of self-disgust.

Ian, like most other ambitious young Scots, had taken the high road to London – although as a railway buff he probably took the night sleeper – and was making his way on Harold Evans's Sunday Times. He commissioned me to pursue the mafia bosses of some exploited potato-pickers near Humbie, a difficult request since I was (like him) a non-driver. But in those pre-Wapping days, expense was no object to a Fleet Street paper: I hired a car and driver for the jaunt, visiting farms and bothies throughout the Lothians. The Humbie mafia proved elusive – I think the Observer got to them first – but my only experience of "investigative" reporting was enormous fun; I could see that I might become addicted to this fashionable form of journalism which combined high expenses with an innocuous social mission and the occasional car chase.

Next Ian ordered a contribution to the paper's special issue celebrating the coming of North Sea oil, a request which had me over a barrel. (Readers are requested to excuse this weakness for puns.) Disgracefully, I hadn't heard much about North Sea oil. But that was all right; I was to concentrate on the local angle, the rise and fall of shale oil. My soft little essay with its whiff of post-industriana was bowdlerised in order to suit the upwardly-mobile nerds who bought Mr Evans's campaigning rag. And so came to an abrupt end my short career as the paper's Scottish stringer.

The research was useful later, however, when I co-operated with my Kirknewton friend, T.L. (Tom) Hardie, a socialist of the Tony Benn school, in compiling a short history of the parish. In our chapter, "The first oil boom", we wrote critically about the "disagreeable results of industry" on a rural landscape.

This prim tone gave the wrong impression. In fact I was as romantically drawn to the dirty, primitive, but not quite vanished shale industry – for we still had bings scarring the landscape – as many modern socialists are attracted to dying or derelict pits, and for the same discreditable reasons of working-class nostalgia. The very names of the oil villages, Broxburn and Tarbrax, Breich and Pumpherston, evoked a lost sense of community naturally appealing to the left-winger's idealistic mentality. But these places must have been hell on earth for the people who lived in them.

At the height of the Lothians oil boom (1865), there were more than 100 works in operation and the industry employed 10,000 men. Then cheap foreign imports flooded the market, precipitating a severe cut in prices, the laying off of workers and the closure of most of the mines. By 1873 only 30 were left. Few booms have been shorter or more brutal in their effect.

Now it was 1973 and Scotland stood on the threshold of a new oil boom. In the media babble only a few quirky souls like Ian Jack remembered that we had been here before and that there might be lessons to be learned about the exploitation of finite resources and the destruction of traditional ways of life for temporary gain. Much later, he gave his brilliant collection of journalism an apocalyptic title. He called it Before The Oil Ran Out.

In an early assignment as the BBC's Edinburgh reporter, I watched the first North Sea oil flow into a Grangemouth pipe while Raymond Baxter, the ex-RAF wallah who was wheeled in for grand occasions of a scientific nature, masterminded the live outside broadcast from some BP nerve-centre in Aberdeen.

This broadcast, transmitted nationally, was considered so

important that Scotland could not be trusted to manage it and London took over – a neat metaphor for the southerly direction of the oil revenues themselves. I was summoned to a "planning conference" at White City with a keen young O.B. producer, who organised the whole affair as he might have overseen a military manoeuvre. The languid Baxter showed scant interest in the visiting provincial; is it only my imagination or did he really address me as "dear boy"?

On the big day, the oil did not so much gush as trickle. I managed to scoop a little of it into a phial and held it to the camera, the British economic miracle safe in my hands. I kept that phial, which has been transferred from house to house as reverently as a family heirloom. Its contents have not quite evaporated yet.

The North Sea bubble challenged at once the familiar argument that we were too poor for self-government, which the nationalists had always disputed anyway, and the SNP adopted a new slogan, "It's Scotland's oil". This was a potent message, though almost as crude as the stuff flowing into the Grangemouth refinery. It asserted what many Scots saw as their natural proprietorial rights to a valuable natural resource while exposing the injustice of Westminster control over the receipts. For the first time the SNP could claim that we would be better off on our own and have some expectation of being believed.

"It's Scotland's oil", a show which would run and run, had its first performances in a succession of press conferences in party headquarters, a crummy basement on the edge of Edinburgh's new town. The long-term inmates included Willie Wolfe, the craggy CND-er who had chaired the party through thick and thin, and Donald Bain, a bearded research officer of persuasive intelligence. I came to know these patriotic rooms as well as anybody – with the singular exception of George Millar, a bulbous-nosed agency reporter, who asked the awkwardest questions in a way which made even the dullest room explode with laughter.

The frequency of SNP press conferences was something of a joke in the Edinburgh media and Donald Monro, the lugubrious news editor in Queen Street, might have suggested to our Glasgow masters that we stop attending them so faithfully. If he had, the idea could not have been taken up. The BBC viewed the nationalist prospect – I almost wrote "threat" – seriously and did nothing to discourage my regular interviews with nationalist apparatchiks. In contrast, I cannot remember ever interviewing the Tory Secretary of State at that time, the almost invisible Gordon Campbell.

One day I bumped into Willie Wolfe outside the BBC studios. "The thing about you, Kenneth," he said mischievously, "is that no one would be able to guess which party you support."

If this was a fishing expedition, Willie would have found me an unappetising catch. I was one of Labour's silent if disenchanted Scottish majority, sceptical enough to be intrigued by the nationalists but repelled by their materialistic approach. Where were the party's policies on education, the law, local government, the arts? What was its broader vision for Scotland? Did it have one? The cultural case for independence which, properly argued, might have tempted Labour's more thoughtful supporters into the nationalist camp went by default – swamped by the one-dimensional oil campaign with its ruthless appeal to the tartan pocket. A Scottish parliament, if it was ever to rise in Edinburgh, would have to be built on a foundation more intellectually credible than a boom which might last 30 years at best. But I didn't confide these eccentric opinions to Willie Wolfe. Instead I said, trying not to sound too pompous, that it was better if we BBC chappies stayed above the battle.

"It's Scotland's oil" appealed to the electorate's baser instincts and the SNP "bandwagon", as the papers called it, began to roll – unstoppably, many thought. It was given a further push by the Tory government's bad faith in failing to deliver the Scottish Assembly which Edward Heath had promised in his "Declaration of Perth" following Sir Alec Douglas Home's devolutionist report.

Inept as it was, I recall the 1970-74 Heath administration with a certain affection. It was probably the last before public relations people (who were later better known as "spin doctors") started to exercise their undue influence on the conduct of government. We were still living in an age when a BBC reporter could ring the Foreign Secretary at home, actually get through to him, and fix an interview without reference to, or authority from, the shadowy ranks of "advisors". Of course we were not dealing with any old Foreign Secretary. We were dealing with Sir Alec, the last of the political gents.

Apart from Scotland's oil, the preoccupations of my professional life during the middle years of the Heath government were swine vesicular disease, a fatal malady affecting pigs, and Icelandic cod wars. Sir Alec was the world expert on cod wars. As a Borders farmer, he probably knew a thing or two about swine vesicular disease too, if only I had thought to ask him.

It was at London's bidding that I called him at the Hirsel, his country seat, one pleasant Sunday afternoon.

"I'm so sorry to disturb you..."

"Not at all. I was just doing a spot of gardening."

"We seem to have another Icelandic cod war."

"Yes, I'd heard. Damned nuisance."

"I wonder if you would mind coming to Edinburgh for a studio interview with me? I know this is short notice, and very inconvenient. It's for the national news, you see, otherwise I wouldn't have dreamed of bothering you."

"It'll be a relief not to have to do the garden. When do you want me there?"

Reliable on cod wars, hot on cold ones, Sir Alec was less agile on the subject of Scottish self-government. When I interviewed him in 1987, I reminded Lord Home, as he had by then become, about his long-buried Assembly idea. He replied with disarming vagueness. Ah, well. The prospect was clumsy and he had recommended it without enthusiasm. Simply hadn't caught on. So what would he recommend instead? "Ministers moving around Scotland explaining policy," mused the elder statesman. Michael Forsyth, the left's new bogeyman, as a missionary to the socialist heartlands – the messiah of Monklands? This was surely beyond the ingenuity of even Central Casting.

In 1974 Forsyth was a 20-year-old undergraduate at St Andrews and, as president of the university Conservative association, in serious training for his starring role as scourge of the chattering classes. But every age needs a bogeyman called Michael. In 1974 we had ours. He entered stage left, read the Daily Worker, and never missed the General Assembly of the Church of Scotland (a very Scottish combination, that). I refer to the dentist's friend, Michael McGahey.

At the height of his powers as a magician, McGahey was

capable of closing down the television at 10 o'clock every night and plunging millions into darkness. In that extraordinary winter of coal strikes, power cuts and three-day weeks, when Heath needlessly took on the miners and lost, I saw less of the SNP's bunker and more of the NUM's administrative coal-face in Hillside Crescent. A prickly operator, McGahey never disguised his contempt for the capitalist media and delighted in making life as difficult as possible for television reporters. A beguiling mixture of the bloody-minded and the calculating, he would sometimes spurn interviews, declaiming the iniquities of the Tory government from the platform and challenging us to use what he had to say. Avoiding any awkward questions, McGahey was thus a superb manipulator of the medium he professed to despise.

His deputy Bill McLean was a more emollient communist, which is another way of saying that unlike McGahey he regarded journalists as members of the human race. After one of the leader's confrontational press conferences, McLean paused to chat with me on the steps of Hillside Crescent. "The trouble with all this," he sighed, "is that I'm missing my golf." I left to film an interview with an Edinburgh candle-maker, one of the few businesses still working overtime.

Covering the "Who governs Britain?" election of February 1974 was oddly exhilarating. The sudden blackouts, the industrial chaos, the gravelly menace of McGahey's oratory contributed to an atmosphere of incipient anarchy, the feeling that anything might happen. In such an unpredictable climate, even the BBC's profiles of the "key marginals" acquired an extra urgency. These painful exercises in political "balance" – dread word – were a tedious chore for any reporter of inquiring mind, indeed almost a negation of what journalism should be about. Circumscribed as we were by the requirement for strict impartiality, I was instructed to give each of the candidates his/her allotted share – 90 seconds and not a second more (or less).

As a rule the first of the candidates would slum it for the cameras in welly boots by a farm gate – factory gate in the case of an industrial constituency – the second would chat up some aged constituent (the deafer and dumber the better), the third would whizz around the neighbourhood in a car. Each would be asked to reflect in appropriately sombre tones upon what Mr Benn called

The Closing Headlines

"the ishoos" and the general threat to democracy as we knew it.

All this safely in the can, the reporter would straighten his hair, don his parka and film several takes of a piece-to-camera from the town square. Take 1 would be obliterated by the overhead whoosh of a low-flying jet. The tactical appearance of the village idiot would ruin Take 2. Just as he was finishing Take 3 – "So it looks like a close-run thing here in Ecclefechan" – a small child would do something disgusting in the background. Really, the format could not have been simpler. Yet it often led to Trouble.

The trouble in Berwick and East Lothian was the chippy personality of John P. Mackintosh, a Labour intellectual and devolutionist, who was defending the inevitable "razor-thin majority" against a smooth young Tory, Michael Ancram, a scion of the Scottish aristocracy. I was disappointed that we didn't hit it off: Mackintosh, a gifted thinker of the Left, should have been a role model, not that anyone had invented role models in 1974. We made him "the one in the car". He lost, but regained the seat nine months later.

Then I flew to Orkney where Jo Grimond, the Liberal member since the year dot, was believed to be fighting for his political life. How the BBC formed this bizarre view I never discovered. It was not an opinion widely shared in Kirkwall, where people looked on Grimond's reign as they might a monarch's, to be terminated only by death or voluntary abdication. This made the reporter's task a delicate one. When I rang his agent I avoided using the loaded word "marginal". But the diplomacy failed: Grimond decided to play hard to get. His office offered one lame excuse after another until I started to panic. I knew, they knew, and Grimond knew that, under the rules, there could be no film without him. Finally word reached us that, if we turned up at the airport on his return from some outpost of Joland, he might, just might, spare us a few minutes from his crowded schedule.

I am tall, but The Great Grimond was a hero of Nordic stature. For once, I was dwarfed. To begin with, he claimed to know nothing of our repeated requests for an interview. The BBC? Who? What? I had experienced this before with a certain type of public figure: it was the important man's distracted air, not to be taken too seriously. I persisted, and with a show of put-upon "all right, if you must" reluctance he gave in. He *supposed* so.

Before he could change his mind we set the camera rolling and I asked him what he regarded as the "ishoos" of the campaign. He answered fluently and well, but I noticed that he addressed all his remarks above my head to some distant part of the Kirkwall runway. Not once did our eyes meet. "Bastard," I thought, smiled sweetly, and thanked him for his time. When I was compiling the first edition of a biographical book called Who's Who in Scotland many years later, I sent Grimond a questionnaire. No reply. Surprise, surprise.

On polling day, I was to present Reporting Scotland from Edinburgh, rest for a few hours, attend an election night briefing in Glasgow, take a camera crew to some factory for "vox pop" reaction to the results, and return to Queen Margaret Drive to present a breakfast-time round-up of the overnight declarations. In honour of the occasion, I bought a splendid jacket with loud checks which "strobed" spectacularly when they hit the screen.

Foolishly I skipped the few hours' rest and went with Alec Maclean, the studio manager in Edinburgh, for "just the one" to a seedy pub off the St Andrew's Square bus station. Alec, younger brother of the director of An Comunn Gaidhealach, was a socialist of like mind and "just the one" turned into a marathon session of extended toasts to any Labour politician who entered our befuddled heads. By the time we parted the polls were about to close.

Willie Wolfe would not have been proud of me that night. At the factory I rather gave the game away by siding shamelessly with the proletarian brothers who cheered Edward Heath's defeat. Not that anyone "back in the studio" noticed; or if they did, they weren't saying. In the middle of the night I startled Bob Christie, a continuity announcer, by greeting him effusively in a Queen Margaret Drive corridor.

"Isn't it (burp) great, Bob? Isn't it (hiccup) bloody marvellous?"

"What is, Ken?"

"Dear old Harold. He's back! He's back! (Burp, hiccup)."

The tearoom near the entrance had been converted into a hospitality suite – an all-night pub where the great and the good drank vast quantities of whisky at the BBC's expense. From time to time a production secretary spoiled the party by selecting a tame pundit or "spokesman" for Donald MacCormick's studio panel.

But as night turned to morning and the birds of Great Western Road began to twitter, the number of twits in the tearoom dwindled. Some drifted away in taxis, others slept where they sat, a few were so hopelessly inebriated that only a producer of rare daring would have used them.

By 6am, I had pretty well sobered up. Sober enough, anyway, to notice that two minutes before the programme was due to begin, the adjoining seat reserved for our political guest was empty. I implored the gallery to fetch someone – anyone – to talk to me. Still nobody. With seconds to spare, I nipped smartly into the sorry remains of the tearoom, grabbed the only semi-presentable MP, and returned to the studio to introduce my jacket to the viewing public. I hope the three OAPs in Wick were impressed.

How media coverage of General Elections had changed even in eight short years. On the night of Harold Wilson's landslide in 1966 the Glasgow Herald sent me to cover the count for several of the Glasgow seats. There were no cameras then. As I nipped out for a smoke between declarations the victorious member for Gorbals, Alice Cullen, followed me downstairs. She was not surrounded by cheering supporters or excitable television interviewers demanding her "reaction". She was alone and going home to her bed like a sensible wee Glasgow wifie. Mrs Cullen even appeared to be carrying a shopping bag.

I returned to the hall and found a distraught figure pacing the corridors. He was smoking furiously and muttering to himself. I wondered at first whether he might be suffering from some mental disorder. "I've lost, I've lost," he was chanting, "lost, lost, lost." In the dim municipal light I perceived that he was none other than Teddy Taylor, the sitting Conservative for Glasgow Cathcart. Teddy did not lose – not that night. Nor was he troubled by the blandishments of television. He was allowed to bite his nails and smoke himself half to death in decent privacy, well away from people asking him how he felt.

In February 1974, unlike 1966, there was no landslide for "dear old Harold", but a Labour government nevertheless, quickly followed by a compromise in the coalfields. The political implications of a newer source of energy had not been a major issue in a campaign which was inevitably dominated by a national (i.e. UK) crisis and the desire of most people to get the country back to work. However, in the second General Election of that year, the mind of the electorate was not so distracted and the SNP's oil card produced a Scottish result of seismic significance:

Labour 36.3%; SNP 30.4%; Conservative 24.7%; Liberal 8.3%.

Picking up almost a third of the popular vote, the nationalists won 11 of the 71 Scottish seats – an astonishing performance which had foreign journalists and TV crews jetting into Edinburgh's small-town airport for the independence party. So it was "the world's press" of popular fable, along with the usual local cynics, who assembled to hail the SNP's new team in an upstairs room of the Caledonian Hotel one crisp October morning. They had even handed us an irresistible caption for the picture..."The first 11". For a small country so mad about football, the figure seemed uncannily right.

The parliamentary party sat rather sheepishly at a long table framed by a wonderful perspective of Princes Street stretching almost as far as the old Royal High School which, unknown to any of us, the Labour government would soon earmark for a Scottish Assembly. Oh, bright new day!

The illusion faded when one scrutinised the team: George MacDonald Fraser's old pal, Mrs Ewing, sporting her don't-mess-with-me grin; her future daughter-in-law, Margaret Bain, a pleasant young teacher married, for the time being, to researcher Donald; a Stornoway councillor, Donald Stewart, of slow Hebridean reassurance; George Reid, a studio-smooth TV journalist; and a Dundee lawyer, Gordon Wilson, who had been put in as skipper. Bless my soul, there too was a former Scottish Council colleague, Douglas Crawford – not, after all, the businesslike Tory I had always assumed.

The others with one exception I forget. The exception was a man called Henderson, who invited me for a drink afterwards in the Cally bar. He was extremely affable and, judging by his sentiments on matters of the day, right-wing.

As I left the hotel some words of Tyrone Guthrie, the Irish director, came back to me. What, I asked him, was wrong with us? Why had we not been able to produce a Scottish national theatre? Because, he replied, there had been in Scotland "a lack, a very definite lack, of personalities". He was talking about the 1920s when he worked here. Surprisingly little had changed.

4

Wizard prang

Running a news desk is not an occupation for anyone of a sensitive or squeamish disposition. One morning the duty editor in Glasgow went almost purple with anticipation as he noted the details of some road accident. "How many dead?", he asked breathlessly. The exact figure was not available yet. But it seemed bad (or, from our point of view, good); with luck we might have a disaster on our hands. He slammed the phone down and began diverting cameras and reporters to the scene. Seldom had I seen a man so innocently happy in his work.

I went to the tea bar. When I returned half an hour later, he was deflated; his boyish enthusiasm had evaporated. "What's wrong?", I asked. "That motorway pile-up," he said. "No deaths, after all. Hopeless."

The news editor in Edinburgh, Donald Monro, was a phlegmatic character by comparison and viewed the excitable atmosphere of the Glasgow office with a sour detachment which I generally found fairly agreeable. However, as a former Sunday Post man, Donald betrayed a residual weakness for "human interest" stories of a rum character. On the rare occasions when he became animated by events, I knew to expect the worst. It might mean that a Gorgie housewife had set fire to her husband's nose or that a Portobello granny had landed a job as a nightclub bouncer. Once, coming off the phone from Glasgow, he was actually laughing. What fresh hell was this?

"You're to represent Scotland in the Nationwide air race," he announced with obvious delight.

"The Nationwide what?"

"You're to be the reporter on the Scottish plane."

"But I don't like flying."

"Don't be a spoilsport," insisted Donald. "It'll be tremendous fun. A wizard prang!"

Unlikely as it seems now, 20 years ago the Scottish news was enclosed inside the wrapping of a confection called Nationwide, a London-based topical affairs slot. Each of the regions – and the BBC regarded Scotland as a region just as it regarded the Midlands and South-East of England as regions – "opted out" after an omnibus introduction from London, did its own thing, then switched back to the Nationwide studio for items of "general" interest.

This was not only insulting to Scotland's sense of cultural separateness, but unsatisfactory in broadcasting terms. Unlike its pot-boiling equivalents south of the border, Reporting Scotland at least made an attempt to report the news seriously, if rarely in sufficient depth. It simply did not conform to the Nationwide demand for "light" magazine journalism. Yet the schizophrenic format met little if any resistance from the BBC's weak-kneed Scottish management. London, even when hopelessly wrong, always knew best.

The facetious tone of the English regional presenters grated on Scottish nerves, yet regular brief exposure on Nationwide could enhance a career. One Stuart Hall, a favourite with northern women of a certain age, gravitated to It's A Knockout, a network series which indulged the English taste for physical humiliation, and is now often quoted as one of the worst television programmes ever made. Appearing in the same slot as people like Hall made me wince in self-reproach, but an invitation from Nationwide could not be easily repelled. One year they demanded to know my tip for the Grand National. I scanned the field for the horse least likely to succeed and selected a rank outsider called Charles Dickens. The literary mare came in third. I forgot to back it.

Now, God help us, they were staging an air race and I was one of the chosen. Worse, it would be "bad form" and "letting the side down" to decline; I was expected to feel honoured. I rang home to tell Margaret and, uncharacteristically, she burst into tears. A premonition? If it was, we became resigned to it. In a perverse way, I even started to look forward to the experience.

The night before, I met the pilot and navigator over dinner in a Glasgow hotel. They were experienced aviators as well as convivial company, and as they outlined the arrangements I felt reassured by their air of calm authority and confidence. We were to take off from Glasgow Airport and fly to Biggin Hill, the Battle of Britain station in Kent, arriving in the early part of the afternoon. Simultaneously our competitors would be setting out from airfields in other parts of the country. Each team would be awarded points for visiting other airports along the way, and the presenter on board would be the team gofer, dashing back and forth to air traffic control to get the logbook stamped. It all seemed perfectly dotty, but as one of the fitter Nationwide presenters I rather fancied my chances. Had I not finished a game third in the committee race at Kirknewton Gala Day?

The experts turned in early, leaving me in the bar, but a few minutes later the navigator re-appeared. It seemed his earlier withdrawal had been purely tactical. He had navigated the pilot as far as the door of his room, pretended to go to his own room, then nipped back downstairs for a furtive whisky.

"You mustn't worry about tomorrow," he said. I hadn't been worrying about tomorrow, but the instruction not to worry about it was, of course, extremely worrying.

"Take it from me," he continued in the same unsettling fashion, "Sandy [let's say that was the pilot's name] went right through the war without a scratch. Battle of Britain hero, you know. No, no, Sandy won't be taking any chances."

"Well, I'm glad to hear it," said I, knocking back another fortifying dram.

The morning dawned bright and crisp. "It seems to be filthy further south," our pilot reported casually, but I disregarded this ominous alert. By now we were several thousand feet above the Borders in a Piper Cherokee. I was crouched in the back, my long legs compressed against the navigator's seat, and shamelessly enjoying this first jaunt in a light aircraft. "It's marvellous," I yelled to my drinking chum. Indeed it was, for we were flying low enough to see towns and villages come and go before us like so many pieces on a board game. How reassuring Britain looked from where we were.

I did a fair bit of running: I suppose we must have landed at six or seven airports en route. All the way to the south of England the weather stayed fine. And then, with amazing suddenness, it changed to thick fog and driving rain. As we descended over Biggin Hill, visibility was so poor that I was only vaguely aware of strange, threatening shapes just outside the window. Then I realised with a jolt that they must be our rivals from the other Nationwide regions, and that they were perilously, unbelievably, close.

By sheer chance we avoided a mid-air collision and crossed the finishing line. I kept thinking that we must land at any moment. Instead we careered out of control and the pilot, his hands gripping the wheel, uttered a word that I had only ever heard in the films. "Mayday!", he cried. He repeated this over and over again, but still I could not quite believe it. We were barely above ground now, but it was a struggle to see beyond the rain-spattered windows. We appeared to be over a field. Trees, barely discernible though only a few hundred yards ahead, loomed out of the mist and after the trees there were houses. We must hit the trees or the houses and either way we had had it.

Between the time we stumbled into the field and the time we nose-dived into the trees – 90 seconds at most – I knew that I was almost certainly going to die. "How did you feel?" as the interviewers say. Well, I felt all right. A number of cows had gathered for shelter under the trees and I remember that they looked startled to see us and that they didn't scatter until it was almost too late: they seemed rooted to the spot, poor creatures. But the imminent prospect of violent death caused me surprisingly little fear or alarm; instead I thought of the absurdity of human existence. I thought: "What a way to go." Was this how it had been for the brave boys who fought in the Battle of Britain? How farcical that the greying middle-aged man a few feet away had survived all that the Messerschmitts had thrown at him, yet was about to perish in an asinine stunt dreamed up by a few silly people at the BBC.

After the crash, there was an eery silence and several moments of suspended animation. I was imprisoned in the rear seat until the pair in front made a move. "Out, for fuck's sake," I pleaded, and all three of us scrambled to safety. For some reason the Piper had not ignited on impact (later I learned why: there had been no fuel left in the engine). We had been extraordinarily lucky.

The field was sodden, and we sank at once into the mud. We just stood there in the rain, gazing stupidly at our wrecked aircraft with its Reporting Scotland insignia still intact. One of us began to laugh. It was a high-pitched, hysterical laugh, a survivor's laugh, and soon we were all laughing. "Maybe," I said between gusts of mirth, "maybe I should go and report the accident." The melodramatic oddity of the remark provoked further hilarity. Yes, quite. How very droll. And we laughed till our sides ached.

Finally I paddled across the field, climbed a gate, crossed a road, and rang a doorbell. A middle-aged woman answered.

"Our plane has just crashed," I said.

"I saw it come down," she replied in a matter-of-fact, this-happens-a-lot way. "I was quite concerned about you. Would you like a cup of tea?"

"No, but I would be grateful for the use of your phone."

"Who is it you want to call? I could dial the number for you."

"You know, I haven't the faintest idea." I felt incapably drunk.

"You're Scottish," the woman said, smiling. "I've had a play published in Scotland by a firm called Brown, Son & Ferguson. I don't suppose you have heard of Brown, Son & Ferguson?"

"As a matter of fact, I have. I'm a sort of play publisher myself. At least I was before I joined the BBC."

"Oh, really?" She sounded intrigued. "Then perhaps you'd be interested in my plays for Brownies."

After this interesting encounter I returned to the scene. A BBC Land Rover arrived and out jumped one of the producers, Ron Neil, a fellow Scot whose solicitor father had been the business partner of the nationalist, John MacCormick. I had not met Neil before, but he greeted me as warmly as a long-lost brother.

"My God, Kenneth, are you OK?"

"I'm OK. We're all OK."

"Thank God, thank God." He looked rigid with shock.

We were bundled into the Land Rover and driven a short distance to the airbase, where RAF people were muttering darkly about what a balls-up the Nationwide air race had turned out to be and how fortunate that the BBC had not killed off many of its regional presenters at a stroke.

One of the Biggin Hill chaps produced a bottle of whisky. "Get that inside you," he said, "and fly again as soon as you can. It's the only bloody thing for it, I assure you."

So we swallowed Johnnie Walker in generous gulps and the rest of the afternoon passed in a blur. We were not medically examined at any stage and there was no suggestion that a change of clothing might be arranged, although we were mud-encased up to our knees. On the contrary, I was to return to the crash site for a live interview about our "ordeal". By prior arrangement the whole edition was to be devoted to the race, although I got the impression that if Ron Neil had had his way the programme would have been aborted on the spot.

A Nationwide reporter, Martin Young, accompanied me back to the wreck, where a camera had been set up and investigators from the Civil Aviation Authority were buzzing around. An inquiry had been instigated, not that this sensitive matter was raised in the interview. It was still raining hard and I must have presented almost as sorry a sight as the doomed Cherokee.

In the gathering gloom I took a last look at the plane, marvelling that we had escaped alive. Then we returned to base for the prize-giving. The presenters stood in line, Stuart Hall beaming to camera, and Frank Bough, who possessed all the warmth of a frozen haddock, announced that Reporting Scotland, despite its misadventure, had actually won the race. I stepped forward to muted applause and collected a cup. And so the jolly charade was played out to its risible conclusion.

Afterwards, my fellow victors made a quick exit – I never saw or heard from them again – and Ron Neil drove me to London, an uncomfortable journey in wet, filthy clothes. It was dark when we finally reached King's Cross. He handed me a voucher for the Edinburgh sleeper and disappeared into the night.

The crash was biggish news in the Scottish press. The Daily Record gave it the back-page lead with a dramatic picture of the Cherokee. I wandered about the village in a daze, behaving oddly for a day or so, but otherwise seemed none the worse of the experience. At the BBC, Donald showed a kindly concern but no one else referred to my wizard prang; when I mentioned it to senior colleagues in Glasgow, the subject was abruptly changed. It did not occur to me that they were afraid I might cause a fuss and hire a smart lawyer.

And that seemed to be that until, many months later, I received through the post a copy of an HMSO report into the incident. The Civil Aviation Authority censured the BBC for going ahead with the race in defiance of a Met Office warning of severe weather at Biggin Hill. This startling indictment of corporate irresponsibility was not reported by Nationwide, which went on pursuing the wickedness of public bodies with its usual zeal and efficiency.

5

Children of the Pissed

Douglas Kynoch quit abruptly as presenter of Reporting Scotland, and the newspapers said that he had "found God" – presumably not in Broadcasting House, Glasgow, although the Lord is known to perform his miracles in mysterious ways.

Neither of his immediate successors occupied the hot seat for long. Bill Hamilton, a Salvationist with a charming smile which delighted the grannies, returned to reporting and John Duncanson secured a more congenial niche with Grampian Television in Aberdeen. Meanwhile Donny B. MacLeod, the only Scottish news anchorman of star quality, was commuting every week to Birmingham, where he presented a frothy lunchtime slot before his lamentably premature death.

The absence of authoritative faces fronting Scotland's flagship programme, and the stodgy character of the news output, would probably have been overlooked by the BBC's soporific local management had it not been for the new political dynamism. The nationalists were on the march; a Scottish parliament seemed inescapable. But Reporting Scotland – "Revolting Scotland" as it was known to insiders – stayed stuck in a provincial groove.

Donald (Monro) believed that the programme should be renamed "Reporting Glasgow", so outrageous was its West of Scotland bias. Here spoke the Edinburgh man with the Edinburgh man's natural distaste for all things Glaswegian. Nevertheless, there was some truth in what he said. As I languished in a studio as big as a ballroom waiting to recite the next of my desultory "links", Donald (not overworked in the gallery) transmitted sardonic messages into my right ear. "Look at that. Another fire in Maryhill Road. Ho, ho. Wait and see. Next it'll be an OAP falling off a bus in Partick." All too often it was.

The Closing Headlines

Ken Bryson was the Ernest Purdy of the set-up, a troubleshooter who chased fire engines, police wagons and ambulances. It was not his fault if the caption "Ken Bryson reports" heralding a breathless account of some mini-disaster within easy reach of the Botanic Gardens caused a certain amount of snobbish ribaldry over in Edinburgh. What was at issue was the ethos of the programme.

Just as, in the West End theatre, few plays were allowed to last more than two hours for fear of stretching the audience's boredom threshold, so few items in Reporting Scotland exceeded three minutes and the average length was nearer two. A reporter who argued successfully that his story should be treated at length – say, four minutes – was doing exceptionally well and items longer than five minutes were practically unheard of. Pace was the master, but at the expense of context, explanation and – though I hesitate to use the snooze-inducing word – "analysis".

It annoyed me that important events in Edinburgh, of some significance in Scottish life, were brushed off by Glasgow. The General Assembly of the Church of Scotland, of which more in a later chapter, was obviously an irksome irrelevance to our hard-boiled executives who were happy to see it shunted into a siding of its own. Nor was there much enthusiasm for regular nightly reports from the Edinburgh Festival, which were introduced in a lacklustre fashion one year and dropped the next.

If Edinburgh got a raw deal, remoter parts of the country might just as well have been left unexplored by Dr Johnson and his young friend for all the interest that BBC Scotland's news department ever showed in them. Occasionally, if "hard" news was scarce, a reporter would be dispatched to the outer darkness of the Highlands or Borders with a film crew and told to pick up timeless "offbeat" material which would be slotted into the programme on a quiet night. This was called "going on safari". It never occurred to anyone that it might be an insulting way to cover rural Scotland.

In a deferential culture, where the only events of consequence were presumed to happen 400 miles away, the shallow vision of the principal television news programme could be understood if not excused. But Scotland was changing and Scots were thinking more deeply about their identity and their future. Although

Matthew Spicer's current affairs unit did some excellent work, the day-to-day journalism from Queen Margaret Drive had a pedestrian flavour which failed to match the country's more adventurous spirit.

Out of harm's way in Edinburgh it was easier to scorn the inadequacy of the product. I was happy there and had no wish to return. I certainly didn't miss the blokeish Glasgow newsroom with its talk of snooker, women and cars. But there were more positive reasons for preferring Edinburgh. The capital city was where it was at or likely to be in the near future. Our studio had just been "colourised", startling viewers who imagined that I had blonde hair – for so it looked in monochrome – rather than a thatch of premature inherited grey. The Sunday Post, bless it, ran a feature about my spectacular ties, which could now be properly appreciated, and I had become a minor local personality, much in demand for church fetes, drama festivals, and the less libidinous type of after-dinner speaking. Above all, it suited me to be a solo operator with my own clearly defined territory.

But when the call came – not from God but from George Sinclair, the next best thing – I would have been a fool not to have heeded it. After years of biding his time George was working himself into position "A" in the news hierarchy and determined to transform Reporting Scotland into a more credible programme.

The played-out format of multi-studio presentation was to be abandoned and Reporting Scotland would henceforth be presented from Glasgow alone (much to Donald Monro's chagrin, needless to say). Mary Marquis, who combined glamour with a sharp intelligence, would alternate as presenter with me, and we would be guaranteed substantial studio interviews. Better still, in the weeks when I wasn't required in the studio, I would enjoy a free hand as a roving reporter compiling just the sort of in-depth film which was sorely lacking at the moment.

I agreed to leave Edinburgh, though not without misgivings: George's plan sounded too good to be true. In fact, the studio interviews materialised as promised and every other week I travelled within Scotland more or less as I wished, assuming there was a freelance crew available to go with me. At the end of the week, if I had produced a seven or eight minute film on a subject of my own choice, no one complained. Sometimes I stretched it to eight or nine minutes and still no one complained. What was going on? I decided that it would be tempting providence to inquire too closely. I would simply make the most of this astonishing turn of events while it lasted.

What was going on, though few of us journeymen fully appreciated it at the time, was a revolution – by BBC standards, anyway – in the executive corridors of Queen Margaret Drive. Rattled by the SNP's progress, London had agreed that "something must be done" to safeguard its position in the run-up to home rule, starting with a more vigorous approach to the reporting of the news.

It says a lot – or, if you like, very little – about the status of the BBC's Scottish controllers that I have forgotten the name of the bureaucrat who ran the show when I joined in 1972. He should have been one of Scotland's most prominent public figures or at any rate a familiar face in the newspapers; instead he was virtually unknown, except perhaps to his wife. But all that changed now. In the final weeks of 1975 it was announced that the editor of the Guardian, Alastair Hetherington, would be returning to Glasgow as our new controller.

When the news leaked out, David English, editor of the Daily Mail, told Hetherington: "You're mad. It will destroy you." The words were to acquire a prophetic ring. But like many Scots at that time, Hetherington was convinced that an Assembly with devolved powers, if not outright independence, was inevitable within a few years and that Scotland was about to become one of the most exciting countries in Europe. After 21 years as editor, he had done all he reasonably could at the Guardian. He was 55 years old and needed a change of direction before it was too late. The top post in BBC Scotland with a devolution bill in preparation must have seemed to a man of his gifts the right job in the right place at the right time.

In retrospect, however, Hetherington made two serious errors of judgement. Although "controller" sounded impressive, this grade was not the highest below director-general: the people who held the real power in the BBC were the directors. He should have insisted on directorate status as a pre-condition, for once he was installed it was too late; the lower grade made it difficult to impose his will and weakened Scotland's bargaining position with

London.

His second mistake was to foul his pitch so quickly with Charles Curran, the director-general. It would probably have happened in any case, since Curran disapproved strongly of a non-BBC man in the job and only agreed to the appointment when it was more or less foisted on him by a strong-minded Scottish governor, Sir Michael Swann. But Hetherington and the prickly DG fell out at the first hurdle when the Scottish controller, betraying the liberal instincts of his newspaper background rather than the innate caution of a BBC administrator, prepared a paper recommending fairly significant devolution of power to Glasgow.

Curran, outraged by what he saw as Hetherington's presumption, summoned him to a meeting by radio link. The fact that the Scottish controller was in the middle of a difficult meeting with officials of the Church of Scotland in Edinburgh made no difference – he must return to Glasgow at once for a ritual dressing-down. An account of that embarrassing episode, the beginning of the end though he was only a few weeks in the job, is included in his short memoir, Inside BBC Scotland 1975-1980: a personal view (Whitewater Press).

I got an inkling of Alastair Hetherington's unorthodox style when Malcolm ("Mack") Coupar, one of the senior men on Reporting Scotland, suggested that we put up the idea of a 30-minute feature on the Highland clearances to coincide with some gathering of the clans. The project as Mack outlined it would involve a great deal of travel in the far north with several overnight stops. Yes, this sounded fun after the rigours of a winter in the Glasgow newsroom. But I didn't rate highly the chances of the news department approving it.

"I don't want to discourage you," I said, "but you must know that George [Sinclair] will never wear this."

"George doesn't have to wear it," he replied with a throaty laugh. "We'll go to Alastair."

"Alastair?" For a moment I was mystified.

"We'll sell the idea to the controller."

This was bold. Foolhardy, some would have said. Programme ideas went through the "usual channels" and were not referred directly to the controller by the humble likes of us. Departmental niceties had to be observed, pecking orders respected. No controller of BBC pedigree who understood the Byzantine workings of the corporation would have tolerated our impudence. What the hell: we'd risk it.

Alastair saw us in his room early one evening. I had not met him before, and my first impression was not of the ruddy outdoor man, the Fleet Street editor who had been known to drag bad-living hacks up mountains with only a packed lunch and a flask of tea for consolation. He radiated loneliness.

He was neither warm nor cold in his welcome but listened to our proposal politely and responded with mild enthusiasm. "Ah," he said when Mack had finished. "So it's a sort of Boswell and Johnson re-visited, then?" "Something like that," Mack nodded. I wanted to ask the controller which of us reminded him of Boswell.

The meeting went well, and soon we were discussing the production schedule and possible dates for transmission. Without actually committing himself in so many words, Alastair seemed to be saying: okay, go ahead, you have my blessing.

Afterwards, Mack sounded jubilant. He lit a cigarette and talked animatedly about the project. Obviously he regarded it as a "break" which would enhance his career. I wondered. Among the greyer functionaries who would still be around after Hetherington had gone, his solo initiative was just as likely to mark him down as "unreliable" (the ultimate offence). But I was happy for him and pleased to be the jobbing reporter. We spent hours planning the trip.

When George Scott, the editor of the Listener, was not available to chair From the Grass Roots, a Sunday morning phone-in on Radio 4, I often stood in for Scott, with Malcolm Coupar as producer. On the day of our departure, we got rid of the last caller, threw our bags into the boot of Mack's car, and with a sense of release made for the high road to the Highlands.

"I think we'll call the programme Children of the Mist," said Mack as we headed for the Duke of Argyll's pile at Inveraray. I agreed that this struck the right note of romantic melancholy. The chief of the clan Campbell, whose castle had been ravaged by fire, ushered us into a dank kitchen where I conducted the first interview. From there we drove miles to God knows where. Every day we drove miles to God knows where. But this was all right. Mack had with him a crew (Bob Thomson, Ricky Walker, Chris

Sharman) who had never heard of union hours and preferred to make their own.

We went jauntily over the sea to Skye, staying in the splendid old inn at Ardvasar with its snug bar full of Hebridean malts, most of which were sampled by the end of the first night. The "protuberances" which failed to impress Dr Johnson but would have excited Alastair Hetherington's admiration, were shrouded in mist and Skye lived down to its reputation by pouring non-stop for 36 hours. Conditions for filming could not have been more trying. Poor little us.

Yet the vile weather gave the pictures an appropriately sombre texture for the documentary's tragic theme. As we bumped along dirt tracks to some cleared village, the rain might have been tears of pity for the communities burned out of their crofts. It occurred to me that these abandoned settlements in settings of silent beauty must be among the saddest places on earth. Perhaps they always felt haunted, even on the sunniest days.

We wasted little time in setting up the gear and taking the shots before hastening to the next pub, there to dry out before a peat fire and a warming dram. To Mack's irritation we often had to travel long distances before encountering the civilised facilities which he took for granted in Moodiesburn. Once our producer had to relieve himself in a field cruelly exposed to the elements, and immediately styled himself "the fiendish flasher of Breakish". In a silly way this added to the manic camaraderie of the enterprise. Still giggling over the incident, we stumbled upon Brian Wilson, the radical journalist and future Labour MP, in the bar of the Broadford Hotel. I think Brian thought we were quite mad; he would not have been far wrong.

After Skye, we drove in a long sweep to the vast emptiness of the far north. Mack said that he knew of a good hotel at Cape Wrath. The hotel in that extreme spot did indeed look fairly inviting. Unfortunately it was still "closed for the winter" – this was the week before Easter – and our convoy was ordered to proceed without delay to the neighbouring village of Tongue.

Here, the hotel proprietor assured us that he had not seen a visitor since the previous October. Judging by his startled reaction when we pinged the bell at reception, it was possible that he had not seen a visitor since the previous century.

Could he give us beds for the night? Slowly and curiously, he looked us up and down. Well, it was like this. The bedrooms had not been aired. It would not be right. No, it would not. So – was there anywhere else in the area? A faint smile crossed his impassive features. "Such a question!" it seemed to say. And then he shook his head and shrugged his shoulders with the weary resignation of the Highland hotelier who never ceases to wonder at the unreasonable demands of the modern tourist. A place to stay? How extraordinary!

Darkness falls quickly on the northern coast on a gloomy afternoon in that half-season between the end of winter and the beginning of spring, and the unfamiliar road stretched into a weird lunar landscape as far as the eye could see.

"What now?" I asked the fiendish flasher of Breakish.

"Thurso," he replied in a small voice.

I reached for the map, still sodden from its visit to Skye. "But Thurso's on the other side of the bloody country..."

"Got a better idea?"

We arrived fairly late in the evening, checked into a dingy hotel, and went straight to the bar. By this advanced stage in our Highland odyssey, the producer must have been suffering pangs of conscience; he thought he had "better speak to Glasgow". When he emerged from the phone box off reception, the rest of us were on our second and the hapless Malcolm was chalk-white.

"I have some very bad news," he said.

"Uh?"

"The film has been blacked by the unions."

"You're joking?"

"They say we broke the agreement by hiring a freelance camera for a non-news assignment. We should have used staff."

"Bolshie bastards! How petty!"

"Yeah," Mack agreed in a defeated voice.

We got drunk. By the end of the night we had vowed to resign from the BBC, open a hotel on Skye, and rename our film *Children of the Pissed*. None of this happened. We returned meekly to Glasgow, never visited Skye again, and begged before a shop steward called Bob, whose charity quiz night in Barrhead I later chaired on the strict understanding that one good turn deserved another: the film was unblacked.

6

Dirty tricks

Yet another face appeared as head of news – the third in almost as many years – with the difference that this face was old and distinguished and appeared to have nothing left to prove. Andrew Boyle, founder of the World at One, billeted himself at the far end of the corridor and for all practical purposes let George Sinclair run the show – though without the title.

Boyle's looming presence in the background was baffling. Why was he here at all? Most nights he invited the senior staff into his room, poured generous measures, and talked informally about how the day had gone. He made no serious criticisms of the programme and had few suggestions for improving it. On the face of it he was that familiar BBC figure, the elder statesman coasting to retirement. Yet there was something in his manner which made for uneasiness. While saying little, he observed and listened too vigilantly for comfort.

This is what Hetherington himself wrote about Boyle in his broadcasting memoir: "...Curran asked me to accept him for some months, until other arrangements could be made...Curran said Boyle would help to strengthen the Scottish team...He [Boyle] seemed helpful to the younger news and current affairs staff, though generated little action himself. As long as he knew what was happening, he was content."

Boyle's apparent inactivity is tactfully expressed, but the key reference in the passage is to Charles Curran, who opposed Hetherington's appointment and set out to make his life at the BBC as awkward as possible. If the DG required a spy in Glasgow, Boyle was not without qualifications. (Three years later, he published a sensational book revealing the identity of the so-called "fourth man" of British espionage.)

Some weeks after Boyle's arrival, a paragraph appeared among the media gossip of Private Eye "linking" Alastair Hetherington with a young woman in BBC Scotland. The story was unfounded. But even if a friendship had existed, it would hardly have qualified as an impropriety far less as a scandal: Alastair was separated from his first wife and the woman was unattached. However the item led to the usual prurient gossip in the BBC Club and distressed at least one of the victims, who told me that she intended to sue the magazine. (So far as I know, she didn't.)

As for Alastair, the cruel tittle-tattle probably undermined his reputation among the staff – not seriously, but just enough to put questions in people's minds. Whoever leaked the non-story knew that it would hurt.

Seventeen years later there was an intriguing coda to the incident. In the spring of 1993 I had lunch in London with a political journalist who was curious to hear that I had worked under Hetherington and Boyle. He claimed to have been friendly with Boyle (who died a few years ago). To my astonishment he then brought up the long-forgotten Private Eye story and asked if I knew the identity of the source. "No," I said, "and I don't know anyone who does."

He smiled. "It was Andrew Boyle. He admitted to me at the time that he had leaked it."

"How come?"

"Well, they'd sent him up to Scotland to keep an eye on Alastair, hadn't they?"

If Alastair was indeed the victim of a dirty tricks campaign, as seems highly likely, it throws into perspective his failure to make any real headway with his plans for "mini-devolution" (paradoxically, a phrase coined by Curran). Time and again he argued sensible proposals for giving Scotland more control over its own administration and budget without the need for constant detailed reference to London; time and again he was thwarted by Curran's malevolence and bad faith.

He did, however, succeed in beefing up Scottish news and current affairs output with a series of appointments to new specialist posts. Michael Buerk came north as energy correspondent, and the political irony of an Englishman in the oil job was not lost on the more cynical among us. For Buerk, who claimed no emotional commitment to Scotland, this was a straightforward career move, another step on the greasy pole, and he returned to London when his masters beckoned. Chris Baur as political correspondent was a more sensitive piece of casting. Though a dull studio performer, he knew his stuff and added considerable authority to the BBC's coverage of the devolution debate. Chris was lost to broadcasting when the Scotsman wooed him as deputy editor.

A third specialist post gave Alastair a packet of trouble. He hired Helen Liddell, a researcher at the STUC, for a trial period and sought approval to consolidate her appointment as economics correspondent. London blocked the move because she had an unsuitable (i.e. West of Scotland) voice – though the same administration had no hesitation some years later in appointing as UK political editor someone with a thick Ulster brogue. Helen Liddell, disillusioned by this shoddy treatment, went on to become Scottish organiser of the Labour Party, where an unsuitable West of Scotland accent was a positive advantage. Later she entered Robert Maxwell's employment as his Scottish publicist and wrote a sexy "blockbuster" novel.

Her successor, Peter Clarke, as right-wing as she was left, must have pleased London with his educated vowels. An amusing eccentric keen on restoring leaky castles, Clarke struggled to make his teatime lectures comprehensible to the masses. Still, for a while he was one of the more engaging characters around "B.H."

Among the general reporters, David Scott stood out as the journalist's journalist. Skilled in both newspapers and broadcasting, he wrote terse, muscular prose and had the best contacts in the business, particularly on both sides of the law. Scott played a hero's role in helping to secure the eventual release of the wrongly-convicted Paddy Meehan and produced a long series of rattlingly good "exclusives". His reward for years of brilliant service to the BBC was a peremptory demand to clear his desk when he announced that he was deserting to the opposition as Scottish Television's head of news.

John Milne was another asset, much admired by Hetherington for his steady judgement, and as effective on radio as he was on the box. But the new regime discovered, sometimes to its embarrassment, that newspaper journalists did not invariably transfer well. One recruit created a stir by introducing her first studio report with a cheery "Good evening!" Some of us were amused; George Sinclair less so.

Two spirited women provided a refreshing distraction from the voices in suits, but neither stayed long in a department known for its misogynist tendencies. Fran Morrison, who had the pushiness of the born reporter and a pleasing voice, disappeared south while Fidelma Cook returned to her natural habitat of newspapers, though she too had the potential to develop into a television reporter of unusual character. From that era the only survivor among the women – or for that matter of either sex – is the versatile Paddy Christie, who retains in her speech the unaffected burr of her native Stonehaven.

Although reporters came and went, some with alarming speed, the fact that a journalist of authority held the top job at BBC Scotland during such a critical period in Scottish life made Queen Margaret Drive a stimulating place to work in the late 1970s. News was no longer considered a tedious appendage of drama, documentaries, and the other "important" work of broadcasting. For the first time it was treated seriously, got a proper budget, and enjoyed the resources and confidence to employ journalists with clout.

This creative interval, though enormous fun while it lasted, was of short duration. I would date it from April 1976, when Callaghan succeeded Wilson as Prime Minister and started to push the devolution case, to the referendum of March 1979, when the Scots had their chance and muffed it – a period which coincided almost too neatly with the Hetherington era at the BBC.

There was no doubt that Alastair, like many other intelligent Scots, anticipated Scottish home-rule and relished the prospect. But what would happen to BBC Scotland in that event?

The question surfaced soon after his return to Scotland at a dinner party which he hosted for an eclectic selection of odds and sods. Mary Marquis was there, Alan Thompson (the Scottish governor), a brooding Andrew Boyle, Magnus Magnusson and his wife Mamie Baird, Charles Nairn (who ran the radio newsroom), and a few others. For the first part of the evening my wife had the misfortune to be seated next to Boyle, who was at his uncommunicative worst. Margaret flattered him by asking what he was "writing at the moment". The honest reply would have been: "An exposure of Sir Anthony Blunt", which would have given us a cracking scoop.

Before the pudding, Alastair startled the company by insisting that we change seats. There were a few incredulous chortles, but no, the controller was serious: apparently this was an honourable BBC tradition on such occasions. So we had a game of guest-swapping before settling down to what was obviously intended as the main point of the evening – a discussion of the volatile Scottish political climate and the BBC's place in it.

"Let's imagine," said Alastair, "that on the morning after the next election, we are confronted with a situation in which the nationalists have a majority of the Scottish seats or are pretty close to achieving a majority. What should BBC Scotland's response be? What would we actually do?"

A long silence ensued. Even Miss Marquis, who was known for her irreverent barbs, was struck dumb. Finally, the answer which had eluded all of us, including the chairman of Mastermind, came from an unexpected quarter. Charles Nairn, who knew all about extempore planning from his years on the radio newsdesk, piped up.

"I suppose what we would do," he said haltingly – whatever could poor Charles have in mind? – "would be to invite spokesmen from all four main parties into the studio."

On a severely practical level this was a splendid answer irrefutable in its logic, but it was clearly not what Alastair Hetherington wished to hear from his staff after dining them so lavishly. If we were to sing for our supper, what was required was an aria not a simple ditty. He was challenging us to discourse philosophically on an important issue of public policy. Sadly, we were not up to it.

The SNP had done some radical thinking on the matter. It had told Hetherington that an independent government would set up a Scottish Broadcasting Authority with three television channels, two financed by a licence fee (a larger one than the BBC's, it was acknowledged) and the other by advertising. Under no circumstances would it continue to take the BBC's services, though it would have no objection to buying in BBC programmes, rather as the Irish did.

A question nearer political reality was the future of BBC Scotland in the event of a Scottish Assembly with wide powers which nevertheless stopped short of independence. Would responsibility for public service broadcasting in Scotland then pass to the Assembly – or would the BBC in London go on controlling the purse strings and the key appointments? The Annan Committee on the future of broadcasting, which reported during Alastair's time at Queen Margaret Drive, was emphatic in its view that the BBC should be obliged to do no more than "take note" of what the Assembly said – a phrase with echoes of Lord Reith's celebrated phrase, "I hear you", meaning "I have to listen to this nonsense, but do not expect me for one moment to act upon it."

Annan opposed Scottish Assembly control of BBC Scotland for fear that it would undermine the broadcasters' "independence". Now, this was rich. Hetherington in his first months in office had had to notify 58 different bureaucrats in the south before he was allowed to spend £800 on new titles for programme credits. Incredibly, even the purchase of an extra doorkey for an unmanned studio in Dundee had to be referred to London. If such petty interference in local administration didn't make a mockery of BBC Scotland's "independence" – what did?

Hetherington began with deep misgivings about a Scottish Assembly's likely role in Scottish broadcasting, but his bruising experiences with Curran and the rest of the BBC establishment had altered his thinking. Perhaps by the time of the dinner party he had come round to the view that a degree of separation from London would be no bad thing. Perhaps he privately wondered if anyone around the table shared this instinct. Of course we knew little of his growing isolation, his difficulties with the obdurate Curran, the extraordinary ill-will he was encountering. Only one among us knew, and Andrew Boyle wasn't saying. Yet our collective ignorance did not excuse our collective apathy.

It was that night when I decided that it wasn't going to happen after all. We were not a dumb bunch. Some day people like us would come to be known disparagingly as the chattering classes. Yet, between the game of chairs and the brandy, a question was put about our country's future and we did not wish to address it seriously or even improvise an answer. If we funked such a question, we would surely funk a larger one – shirk from it in sheer terror.

After the party, Magnusson led the way down into the car park, bemoaning his new fame as master of a silly little quiz. Yet a specialist round on "Scottish politics 1974-1979" might be instructive, even in the cold light of a drearier day.

Q.: Why did only 32% of Scottish voters support an Assembly in the referendum of March 1979?

A.: Because we had our usual failure of nerve. Because we secretly prefer to be patronised by London. Because we're a gutless bunch and always will be. Because we don't deserve good men of vision and don't cherish them when they come among us. Because — oh, God, I don't know. Isn't that enough?

C'rrect.

7

Sort of famous

"John Toye!" chanted a gang of Glasgow youths as I crossed their path in a city street. "John Toye! John Toye!" One of the casual indignities of minor fame was to be mistaken – deliberately in this case – for my opposite number on "the other side". The imprecise "Heh, do you no' work for STV?" was not quite so demeaning.

Newsreaders, like star footballers and characters in a soap opera, enjoy a pitifully transient celebrity and memories of John Toye are already fading. Yet there was a time, in that distant day-before-yesterday, when his was one of the more familiar faces in the land. Unlike me he was a genuinely popular figure, a personality of mass appeal. He had been an actor in his youth, perhaps not a very successful one, yet the handsome presenter of Scotland Today wore the easy air of an old-fashioned romantic lead, instantly attractive to women.

Once, when I complained about money, which I was too insecure to do often, George Sinclair attempted to appease me by offering a "facility trip" to Copenhagen. I had not been on such a junket before – at least, not since the intoxicating days of the Falkirk water trip when the local editors and reporters joined the provost and councillors on an annual inspection of reservoirs. There seemed to be a surprisingly large number of reservoirs in the Falkirk area; it is possible that they built a few specially for the occasion.

Of course the inauguration of a direct air service from Glasgow to the Danish capital was in a grander category, but I would have preferred a salary rise, however small, to four days in Copenhagen. I had reached the age of 32 without going abroad and had no particular ambition to start now. Besides, I rarely felt at ease in the company of fellow journalists except when I could choose the company. On both these counts I was something of an oddity.

Half a dozen went on the trip, including John Toye and me, one of the Scotsman's senior reporters, and a pleasant young sub-editor from the Glasgow Herald. A busy programme had been arranged, including a visit to the Carlsberg brewery and dinner with a senior minister in the Danish government. But the talk on the flight over was not about the state of Denmark or British Airways' innovatory links to the Continent. Rather it was about how soon the lads might fit in their first visit to Copenhagen's red-light district, which was reputed to be the most lurid in Europe. (No longer, I understand.)

We were met at the airport by a mini-bus and a courier who would accompany us wherever, within reason, we wished to go. She was a woman in her early thirties, pretty in a pale way, with soulful eyes. She spoke excellent English and was eager to please. John Toye pounced without delay. The two of them sat together on the bus, chatting animatedly, and by the time we reached our hotel she had fallen for his well-practised matinee charm. The rest of the group greeted his accomplished performance with a mixture of envy and amazement.

Dinner that evening with the government minister was not the starchy affair we had anticipated, but relaxed and indiscreet. One of us, pretending to a deep knowledge of Denmark's rampant inflation, asked if the country was not in danger of going off the rails. The politician roared with laughter. "Of course, of course," he agreed. "Absolutely off the rails. But what you must remember about we Danes (pause for dramatic effect)...is that we are all travelling *first class*." It was a marvellous quote. I looked forward to using it. Then I remembered that this was only a freebie (tradespeak for a courtesy trip which is not expected to yield meaningful copy).

Later, I went for a walk with the Glasgow Herald man. We explored the area around our hotel, a seedy quarter of waterfront bars and cafes. The natives were friendly and we soaked up the atmosphere as well as several pints of the local ale. Stepping out into a balmy night, we paused to admire the soft lights of the harbour and began our short stroll to the hotel.

We were stopped in our tracks by a cacophony of sirens. A few yards ahead, a small crowd was crouched over the body of a young woman. She had been knifed by a client only yards from where we had been drinking. No one seemed perturbed by the incident and the police made short work of it. But for me, this was an amazing sight. In all the months as Ernest Purdy's holiday relief I had seen nothing worse than a beating-up in Govan police station. Yet here I was, new in a strange capital, witnessing my first murder. For a few moments I experienced a powerful urge to rush to a telephone and demand "Copy". And then, for a second time that evening, I realised that this was a story with nowhere to go – a scoop without a home.

When we returned, the others had gone to bed – all except John Toye who was drinking with our courier in a corner of the bar. She left soon afterwards and John seemed vexed: perhaps we had interrupted the seduction scene at a crucial moment. Too bad!

Next night, after our tour of the brewery, we visited the offices of Politiken, the left-of-centre Copenhagen daily, and watched the paper roll from the presses. Toye was missing and, as they say in newspaper stories about absconding vicars, it is understood his friend left home at the same time. Nor did he appear for breakfast. But when he was spotted later in the day and one of our party, tongue in cheek, expressed concern for his welfare, he smiled a secret little seducer's smile. In what remained of our time in Copenhagen, he was constantly in the lady's company and rarely in ours.

Without her, John fell unusually silent and morose on the bus to the airport. He turned the dog-eared pages of one of the hard-porn magazines which one of our number, a respectable family man, intended to smuggle out of the country; but did so in a cursory way without enthusiasm. He did not speak of the woman and we parted at Glasgow. I never saw him again, except on those occasions when (too often for my liking) George Sinclair insisted on rewinding his video recording of the opposition's bulletin and we spent 20 minutes heaping derision on STV's attempt to report the news. George's deputy, the admirable Bob Millar, with a furious suck at his pipe, would pronounce it "pathetic" or "feeble" and we would all nod eagerly, longing to be out of the office and home to our neglected families.

A tougher management took over at STV, which declared that it wished to be known in future as "Scottish". More women reporters, some young enough to be called girls, appeared on the screen but there were fewer middle-aged men (and even fewer middle-aged women). John Toye's day was over, though he clung on until they showed him the exit – without unnecessary ceremony, so the papers hinted.

Unknown to me, he went to live in south-west England. His career never recovered. He was lonely and depressed, desperately short of money. One day, he took a gun to his head and blew his brains out. His shocking death was extensively reported in the Scottish newspapers. Some blamed STV – "Scottish" – for murdering him. I scanned the headlines, but I didn't buy the newspapers that day. I had no wish to know the sordid details of John Toye's last years, nor to imagine the tormented soul he must have become. I thought instead of the debonair figure on the bus to Copenhagen, chatting up the girl with the soulful eyes; and of the long bright day stretching ahead for both of them.

There were consolations in not being as famous as John Toye. I was never puffed up by celebrity longer than it took for some geriatric viewer to press his (more often her) wizened features against my nose and demand to know which programme I was "on". Surprisingly often I was mistaken for a sports reporter, and even when they got it right, I was usually dismissed as "one o' they newsreaders".

How I loathed the description. I liked to think of myself as a writer and reporter, not as some puppet spouting other people's words (which, in any case, I reserved the right to change). But the punters – our patronising term for the viewing masses – could not be expected to recognise such subtle distinctions. I learned to smile bravely when people accused me of being a newsreader.

Once I declined to smile and paid a hefty price. We were on holiday in Pitlochry and, since it was very wet, as it often was during our Highland holidays, there was not a great deal to smile about. I queued for lunch in a self-restaurant service near the bus station. For whatever reason – the length of the queue, the weather, the fact that my younger son had just beaten me at putting – I must have appeared even more disenchanted than usual.

When, at last, I reached the head of the queue, the old woman who was serving turned on me. "What right have you got to look so miserable?", she demanded venomously. "A young man like you, a public figure, with a face like that. It's an absolute disgrace."

"I beg your pardon?"

"Look at Sandy Lyle. Such a pleasant young man. Always smiling. Always pleasant. Why can't you be more like Sandy Lyle? Why must you look so miserable?"

After this salutary vignette, I became a devoted follower of Sandy Lyle's smile and, indeed, of that gifted player's career. Though a charming, boyish smile, it struck me as more fragile than his Pitlochry supporter claimed. In the late Eighties, it disappeared for several years and was replaced by a puzzled frown when Sandy's first marriage broke up and he lost form. Later he re-married a Dutch physiotherapist who, according to the sports pages, tickled his toes before they went to bed each night. The massage had a beneficial effect on Sandy's game. Soon, he was smiling again. He is smiling still, though sometimes between gritted teeth, for his game is patchier than it was. At the time of writing, it is by no means certain that he will win automatic selection to the 1993 Ryder Cup. As you may have gathered, I can become a serious bore on the subject of Sandy Lyle and his smile.

Another year in Pitlochry, we were tripping off a bus outside Fisher's Hotel when one of the passengers could restrain her curiosity no longer. She was not malevolent as the last had been: merely loud and aggravating. Had I been one of those Daily Express men who used to stalk holiday resorts dishing out fivers to eagle-eyed readers, she would have been entitled to claim her prize.

"I know who you are," she announced so that all the bus would hear. "You're Kenneth Roy." In response I said nothing but smiled as Sandy Lyle might smile after he has just missed a short putt on the last green for a closing round of 79.

"Aye, I knew it," she said, nudging her companion. "I knew it was you. I just said to her – that's yon boy frae the telly. That's that Kenneth Roy. Mind ye, *she's* never heard o' ye!" (The compliment with the sting in the tail was characteristic). And the bus-pass brigade dissolved into bronchitic cackles.

My wife, who had witnessed variations on this theme for the thick end of five years, decided that enough was enough. "Actually," she said sweetly, "this is not Kenneth Roy. People are always saying he's very like him." With that brilliant stratagem we made our escape.

If I had been rich, I would have bought a black limo, hired socialist Bob as my chauffeur, and cultivated a reclusive image. Instead I earned £6,000 a year, a modest salary even in the mid-Seventies, and would have struggled to afford a car even if I could have driven one. Yet, though far from rich, I was "sort of" famous – not a star with wealth and all its trappings, but well-enough known to be teased by old ladies on buses. A lowering fate.

Over the years I learned to cope, while dreading the almost daily invasions of privacy and the blandishments of my dottier supporters. At least they were fairly innocuous on the whole. Only one to my certain knowledge wasn't.

For a bit of extra cash I occasionally co-presented Good Morning Scotland, the breakfast programme on Radio Scotland, teaming up with the avuncular – how he must detest that adjective – Neville Garden and responding slow-wittedly to the "spontaneous" punchlines of the resident sports reporter, Roddy Forsyth.

One morning, while the admirable Bob Kernohan read Thought for the Day, Gregor Robertson, the studio manager on the other side of the glass, whispered casually into my ear: "Forgot to tell you. There was a policeman here to see you earlier. Said he was from the Met. He'll be waiting for you downstairs at the end of the programme."

As Bob was not yet finished the sermonette, I could not immediately respond to this astonishing piece of intelligence. A policeman? From the Met? He might just as well have announced that a man from Mars had called.

Linking into the next pre-recorded item, I thought with thumping heart of the trap-door in Glasgow High Court which led to the unspeakable horrors of the Barlinnie dog box.

"What does this policeman want with me? Any clue?"

"None," Gregor said flatly.

Sure enough, a man was waiting for me in reception – a short, anonymous Englishman in a mackintosh. He would have been a dead ringer for the eponymous hero of Priestley's An Inspector Calls, the God-like figure who exposes the turpitude of the smug middle-class. And, unlike Sandy Lyle, he was not smiling; he would not have appealed one little bit to the keepers of Pitlochry tearooms.

"We'd better talk in here." Already I was beginning to sound like something out of a detective thriller. I ushered him into Donald Monro's empty office and we stood facing each other across the room.

Solemnly he introduced himself as an inspector something or other from the Metropolitan Police and explained with ominous deliberation that he had come to Scotland to investigate a murder in Clapham. A photofit of the suspect had been widely distributed to police stations throughout London. As a result, a "member of the public" had rung the Met to report that the photofit bore a close resemblance to Kenneth Roy, a newsreader with the BBC.

"Well, does it?"

The man from the Met chose not to answer. Instead he demanded to know where I had been on the evening of – let us say – March 21. Yes, I thought, it's just like this in the films. I told him that I couldn't remember, that I didn't keep a diary, that it was more than likely I had spent the evening at home. He seemed unimpressed. So, he persisted, had I or had I not been in London on the evening in question? Emphatically not. How could I be so sure? Because, I said, it was two years since I had last been in London.

"Look inspector," I said, "this would be hilarious were it not so serious. I am not your man."

"Yes, sir. But is there someone who can account for your movements?"

(I know the dialogue is corny. I wish I could improve it. But this is how it was, m'Lud.)

Reluctantly he produced the photofit. I gazed at it in disbelief. Though roughly the same age, the murderer was an emaciated individual with an abnormally thin face. He looked quite ghastly. If this was me, it was time I hung up my earpiece.

I handed back the picture. "Absurd," I said dismissively.

He neither agreed nor disagreed. There was an awkward silence. Then he made for the door.

"So that's it?"

"We'll be in touch," he said – not, I felt, altogether benevolently.

I heard no more about it. To this day I am unaware whether anyone was arrested or tried for the crime. Perhaps my name remains on file, the suspect they couldn't pin it on, the one that got away. Could someone really have believed me capable of murder? Or had it simply been an act of malice – another of the perils of celebrity? Like all the best mysteries, this one remained unsolved.

8

Canteen characters

In and around Byres Road there were several watering holes frequented by BBC people. The most notorious was the BBC Club with its dipsos, womanisers and shifty hangers-on. Perhaps it has been reformed – in a perverse way it would be disappointing if it has – but at one time it was probably responsible for more broken marriages than any other single address in Glasgow.

If "The Club" had no rivals for miscellaneous sordidness, the Curlers pub was a cheerless alternative – ousted in recent years by the upstairs bar of the Ubiquitous Chip, the Glesca meeja's restaurant, better known to neighbourhood buskers as the Iniquitous Tip. The parlour upstairs has come to be a principal den of hairy West of Scotland dramateurs, self-important producers, pouting PA girls on the make, and the usual entourage of arse-licking hacks and poseurs – in short, Pseud's Corner, Scottish Branch.

The best people were seldom if ever seen in these showy establishments. Come to think of it, the best people were usually only seen in the BBC canteen.

Chic Murray, the comedian, perhaps the most literate Scotland has produced, practically lived in the canteen. When I met him for the first time I felt that I already knew the droll man intimately. Years before, he had been one of my father's favourite acts at the Roxy Theatre, the sweaty fleapit in Falkirk (demolished, of course, to make way for a "shopping centre") where he and his wife, Maidie, topped the bill. My father seldom missed their second house on a Saturday, though how much he remembered of it afterwards was sometimes debatable. I must have been a fairly young child when I attended the Roxy with him, yet Chic Murray's clever use of language and brilliant timing, his manipulation of pace, left a lasting impression.

The Chic Murray I knew was a sadly diminished figure. He suffered from a number of self-inflicted showbiz "problems", he and the long-suffering Maidie had parted, and with the closure of the Roxy and most of the other Scottish music halls, his career had hit the skids. In a building not short of misfits and has-beens, he was among the loneliest. Forlornly reaching out for human companionship, he would have talked to anyone yet almost always sat alone. Poor Chic was regarded as one of the great canteen bores.

After I had left the BBC, I watched with growing horror a more than usually embarrassing Hogmanay show. It was being broadcast "live" (after a fashion) from the Gleneagles Hotel, a popular rendezvous of pot-bellied American golfers with tartan trews, but commandeered on this occasion by some extremely tired and emotional heid-bummers of Scottish business. Between their tables weaved a number of performers in various states of disarray, climaxed by the appearance just before (or it might have been just after) the bells of an uncertain and rambling Chic Murray. Some kindly soul had decided to give him one last break. Some kindly soul had been misguided.

So gifted an artist – a word not to be used lightly – ill-deserved such an undignified curtain, and when he died several weeks later, inevitably the obituaries were coloured by the dismal memory of his final appearance. As I write, his reputation is being upwardly revised: a play celebrating the work of Chic Murray has opened in Glasgow. Through it, a new generation may come to appreciate what a comic master he was, though I doubt whether any actor could recapture the peculiarly dry flavour of the original.

I would unhesitatingly have made Jameson Clark my next canteen character until I realised that I could not conjure up a picture of dear Jimmy actually in the canteen. But I will give him a table of honour there anyway. If he was not a habitué, he somehow looked as if he should have been.

Coming face to face with Jameson Clark, it was almost a shock to discover that he was not dressed in constable's uniform. In the legendary Whisky Galore – shown so often on television that it was almost part of the furniture – he played the ponderous village bobby as well as a ponderous village bobby has ever been played.

Indeed he was more like a policeman than any real policeman. He could be said to have re-created a Scottish type which owed its appeal to the need for comfort and reassurance. He represented the power of rural myth over urban nightmare.

Jameson, an Ayrshireman and proud of it, had in his youth appeared in a celebrated production of Barrie's The Old Lady Shows Her Medals by the Ardrossan and Saltcoats Players: not the original production, winner of the world cup for amateur drama in New York, but a later version which toured extensively throughout Scotland. He made a successful transition to the professional ranks, pretty well cornering the market in couthy character Scots which he, being a couthy character Scot himself, delineated quite naturally.

But there was more to Jameson Clark than his series of engaging cameo roles. He was a genuine example of a very rare combination – the actor/journalist – and if not the BBC's first television reporter in Scotland, he was certainly among the earliest. As Peter Black recorded in his personal history of the BBC, The Biggest Aspidistra in the World: "In 1952 Cecil McGivern launched Special Enquiry, the most ambitious current affairs series yet attempted, with a hard-hitting programme filmed in the slums of Glasgow with Robert Reid in the studio calling in Jameson Clark as reporter in Glasgow. This kind of thing established a basic technique of television reporting which proliferated into a score of later programmes."

By the 1970s, Jimmy had declined into a slow, rather breathless old age, scratching a living from the radio table in the Glasgow newsroom. Most days Charles Nairn dropped a crumb or two, and Jimmy trotted off with a Uher (tape recorder) to compile some filler for the Radio 4 Scottish opt-out which was the height of BBC Scotland's ambitions in those days.

The veteran contributor loved to talk nostalgically and at length about past glories, as old stagers are entitled to do, but most of the Glasgow newsroom's main chancers, who might have learned a little about the craft of broadcasting by listening to him, thought of him as a joke figure, a relic of the Home Service who had outstayed his welcome. As he lumbered about the newsroom, pathetically grateful to be still part of "the team", he was a reminder of gentler times. I must not exaggerate: he was also a fearful gossip, not always to be trusted with a confidence. Nevertheless I loved him.

Another Clark, Bob, really was a canteen character. He had spent too many years as a schools producer, an almost subterranean activity in the BBC, and should have been promoted to a more intellectually rewarding job. Like so many others, he appeared to be marooned in mid-career and resigned unhappily to his fate. For this reason, or other reasons, he was the most sardonic producer in Queen Margaret Drive – against stiff competition, at that – but he was also a man of wit and intelligence, oddly sociable in a dark way, and striking to look at. Tall, stooped and balding, with a penchant for chain-smoking from a filter, he would have been a caricaturist's gift.

At his invitation I scripted a few schools series. The work paid poorly at first, but the programmes were recycled term after term for each new supply of brats and, years later, they were still yielding small repeat fees. One morning my wife happened to glance in the window of a TV rental shop and was startled to see her husband's face animated on no fewer than nine screens. A few days later another modest cheque arrived. Good old Bob Clark.

Tom Wright, the television script-writer, whose work for the stage included a solo play about Robert Burns which helped to make John Cairney's name (Wright and Cairney later fell out badly), used the canteen as a study. Most days he scribbled in a corner, surrounded by BBC coffee cups, and few dared to disturb the Wright muse in full flow. He had a gentle, amused face, but I do not remember ever exchanging a word with him. It was his office, after all.

Wright worked for Pharic Maclaren's drama department; at any rate, everyone assumed that it was Pharic's department. As we were to discover, however, this revered man was never officially head of drama – a post which did not exist until later – but merely a senior producer, a lower form of life.

When I joined the BBC Pharic was at the top of his form, his creative inspiration and love of Lewis Grassic Gibbon's lyrical novels of the Mearns having given birth to the drama series which I still believe is BBC Scotland's greatest achievement – his dramatisation of Sunset Song with Vivien Heilbron as Chris. It is rare indeed for television to recapture the internal nuances of a novel, but such was Pharic's instinctive feeling for the book and the vanished Scotland which it evoked that amazingly little was lost in its transfer to the screen. He then made the mistake of adapting the other parts of the Grassic Gibbon trilogy which were not so good even in their original form. If anything should have stood alone, near-perfect in its delicacy, it was the BBC's production of Sunset Song in 1971-72.

The director of programmes in London, Alasdair Milne, who was soon to succeed Hetherington's bête-noire, Curran, as DG, decreed with his knowledge of Scotland – he had been Scottish controller – that a head of drama should be appointed. To quote Hetherington: "...Milne felt that because Pharic had to move in a wheelchair he was not fully fit to handle a wide range of programmes."

Pharic Maclaren did indeed "move in a wheelchair" – it was a privilege for some of us to hold the canteen door open for it – but better a man who moves in a wheelchair and creates Sunset Song than a hundred able-bodied men who walk through the canteen door unaided and bring forth Rab C. Nesbitt, Taggart, or any of the other grotesque misrepresentations of Scottish life. In any case – to dignify Milne's patronising objection with a practical reply – a head of drama could perform the job's essential tasks (strategic planning, commissioning) just as competently from a wheelchair as from any other make of chair.

The charade of a "board" (BBC-speak for an interview panel) went ahead. Pharic Maclaren applied in effect for his own job and didn't get it. One Rod Graham came north and supervised a number of glossy serials of indifferent quality. Pharic, meanwhile, was seen less often in the canteen. He died a few years later.

Happily, Archie Macpherson is still among us, but not with the BBC, which made the serious error of dispensing with his services when it had no one of equal capability to replace him. The sports commentator, though not too proud to break canteen bread with the lowlier orders, was known as "difficult" (almost as heinous an offence as "unreliable"). True, he shared with The Great Grimond a lofty tendency towards the rest of the human race, except when it was called Jock Stein, whom he idolised. To some, putting it roughly, he was a stuck-up big customer. Personally I always found him endearing.

In my studio weeks on Reporting Scotland, I awaited with gloomy anticipation the Friday night ritual when the better goals from the previous Saturday were re-assembled into a patchwork of "highlights" for Archie's sports slot. This was not only a lazy time-filler, but gave a misleading view of Scottish football. The BBC's film editors, by a process of ruthless selectivity which excised all but a few seconds of goalmouth drama, created an impression of spectacular fluency – an example of television's ability to distort events. Perhaps these snapshots deepened our national mood of frustration when Scotland matches were transmitted in their entirety and we could see that there was less to football than met the eye.

No one could have transformed the Friday sports "package" into respectable journalism, and Archie, who had the larger matter of his Saturday fixture to attend to, simply did the business. But his easy command of a studio was wonderful to behold. He improvised links, mastered last-minute changes to scripts and film sequences, and camouflaged technical cock-ups more effectively than anyone I knew. He was a natural. He might have been born for the medium. He was, however, a martyr to his hair.

In contrast to the Glasgow canteen, its Edinburgh equivalent had the ambience of an arty-fartyish tearoom congenial or otherwise depending on how arty-farty one felt from day to day. Bow-tied classical music producers dallied here between string quartets, and scholarly discussions on the history of the American Indian were conducted over weak tea and chocolate digestives.

The only time it came truly alive was during the three weeks of the Edinburgh Festival, when Joan Bakewell and other imported turns underscored the importance of the event and the inability of Scots to cover it for the network. One year, in a pioneering experiment, I was asked to introduce BBC2's transmission of the opening concert starring Janet Baker, an ordinary wee diva it seemed to this untutored eye. I borrowed a dinner suit from Moss Bros and perched on a balcony of the Usher Hall whispering the names of obscure – to me at least – composers reverentially into a "lip mike", a frightening contraption pressed against one's mouth in order not to disturb the neighbours. I was uncomfortable. The experiment was not repeated.

Despite its unhurried pace, the Edinburgh studio produced good work over the years, particularly in the department of radio plays, with Stewart Conn conducting a one-man campaign to save the national drama from virtual extinction. But there were doubts about the industry of others. The job most of us coveted was "Edinburgh manager", a grand-sounding sinecure which entitled the holder to an office of dignity and charm as well as invitations to many of the best parties, but which seemed to carry few actual responsibilities.

For years the Edinburgh manager was a breezy old buffer from the north-east, George Harvie. Though too nice to show it, he must have been devastated by Renton Laidlaw's departure. A fanatical golfer, George was a supporter of Peter Oosterhuis, a British player of exceptional height with a dodgy swing which often threatened to disintegrate and eventually did. My predecessor Laidlaw, on the other hand, preferred Oosterhuis's great rival, Tony Jacklin, and the pair quarrelled fiercely about the merits of their heroes. Long after Laidlaw had gone, poor George still couldn't accept that his adversary had deserted him. Twice or three times a week he would pop into Donald Monro's office and cry, "Oosterhuis!", an invitation for us to drop pencils and entertain George for the next 30 minutes or so.

This was a nuisance: an agreeable nuisance, but a nuisance. So when friends approached me on behalf of a young graduate with ambitions to break into broadcasting, as friends sometimes did, I vowed to get my own back on George Harvie.

"What's her name?"

"Sheena McDonald."

I had never heard of Sheena McDonald, and if I had been playing by Royal & Ancient rules I would have given my friends the name and address of the BBC's personnel officer and left it at that. Instead I would irritate the Edinburgh manager: repay him for all those hours of Peter bloody Oosterhuis. I would land him with the girl, and hope that she was one persistent operator.

I was not far wrong.

Sometimes, overwhelmed by an acute attack of Oosterhuis or by the Edinburgh preciousness which pervaded other parts of the building, I forsook the canteen and went in search of ordinary drink. Here too the contrast with Glasgow was marked, for there was no pub which you could have called "the" or even "a" BBC pub. So I used the one nearest, the Beau Brummell, where Iain Thorburn, a gifted journalist and deputy editor of the Times Ed Supp, propped up the bar. His companionable talk made me regret that I had ever left newspapers. Good God, I was in danger of becoming a canteen character myself.

9

Mods and blondes

Each May under the reproachful gaze of John Knox's statue in the quadrangle of New College, Edinburgh, a small ritual was enacted (perhaps it still is). The Kirk's new moderator, having received the acclamation of his peers, left the Assembly Hall in order to be interviewed for the BBC television news.

The ritual, though in its essential character unchanging, differed subtly from year to year according to the whim and temperament of the man in the crazy gear. (I will not attempt to describe the costume worn by the Church of Scotland's "first among equals". This would require the skill of an exceptional fashion editor.) The mood was also susceptible to the vagaries of the Edinburgh climate, for no moderator, unless he was more than usually gaga, wished to have his splendid new breeches soaked – even for a spot on the box.

A further risk was that some hitch would sour the dignity of the occasion; something as silly as a fag-puffing spark fooling around with a blonde. For readers unfamiliar with this jargon, a brief glossary: a spark is a BBC electrician, a blonde is a type of television light, and a fag is a plain cigarette smoked by sparks.

Each year my interview with the moderator adhered to a set text; I was as constant as Jeremiah. First I would point accusingly to the latest decline in the Church of Scotland's membership as proof that the institution had lost its way. The moderator would reply unfailingly that, despite the figures, the Kirk was in "good heart" – an off-the-peg C. of S. phrase from the same haberdashery as "going the extra mile". Then we would chew over the topic of the week – say, the gender of God or the proposal to admit a murderer to the ministry. Finally, I would ask the mod about his travel plans – fortnight in darkest Africa, official tour of

Prestonpans fire station, that sort of thing – before wishing him well for his term of office.

Once the Christian gent had gone, we filmed the "noddies". Noddies are shots of the interviewer nodding as if in response to what the interviewee has just said; in fact they are filmed after the event and inserted in the cutting rooms as a visual device enabling the film editor to jump the tedious bits without the joins showing. In short, noddies are a con. Worse, they are an unconvincing con. How often reporters are made to look foolish by the thoughtless editing-in of inappropriate facial reactions at the wrong moment.

I digress, though not much. It was possible with a sympathetic or vigorous noddie to lend extra credence to someone's case, and this I invariably did with the General Assembly interview. At that time I had a genuine affection for the Church of Scotland and a strong belief that it was a force for good in a dislocated culture. I came to recognise that I had been too kind by half. I was so blinded by the Kirk's importance that I failed to ask the only question which should have been asked: "Now tell me, mod, what has all this – the garden party, the Lord High what's-his-name, the morning suits. that fancy dress you're wearing, the hilarious self-importance of the whole occasion – what has all this to do with a carpenter?" I would like to ask it now, but I am unlikely to get the opportunity.

I appeared too late for the moderatorial years of Andrew Herron (1971), the wittiest wee man in the Kirk, and Selby Wright (1972), an old soldier who was known irreverently as the Very Rev. Seldom Right. But I was there in time to greet another mod of military distinction, George Reid (1973), who startled the Assembly some years later by declaring his conversion to unilateral nuclear disarmament, and I stood my ground when David Steel (1974), the politician's father, went into a fearful huff because of one of our technical hitches – was it the spark or the blonde or a bit of both that year? – and indicated that a person of his high office and pressing duties should not be delayed by the likes of us. He went straight into my black book along with The Great Grimond. (I have never had much luck with Liberals.)

The 1975 mod, Portree's James Matheson, with his gentle, almost hypnotic lilt, was a delightful man in every way. Indeed had he not been a senior bureaucrat at Kirk HQ, the notorious

"121", I would have considered James Matheson a saint. His successor, Tom Torrance, dazzled with his theology, but this formidable divine was not one of life's natural five-minute jobs. John R. Gray (1977) – we were advised to remember the "R", perhaps to distinguish him from a small bearded gentleman who succeeded Oosterhuis's friend as the BBC's Edinburgh manager – had an air of pomposity, not as bad as Steel snr., but enough to suggest that he might be put off by erratic blondes. Yet when I met him at an Ayr bus stop after he had demitted office, John R. was amiability itself. I fear the uniform does things to people.

Peter Brodie (1978), a bluff character from Alloa, and Robin Barbour (1979), an academic with a fine brain but a distracting tic, were my last moderators before I took the Devil's shilling and entered commercial radio.

Even the funniest or potentially most controversial moderators tended to be on their best behaviour, and indiscretions were rare. Perforce we looked elsewhere for pleasure: to the gates where the proddy's proddy, Jack Glass, railed agin the Kirk's papist tendencies; to the radio studio where commentary was shared between Johnston McKay, a pipe-smoking, conspiratorial figure who knew everything and everyone, and the unseen Vernon Sproxton (Did He Exist?), whose name suggested some baffling gadget with an incomprehensible manual; or, mischievously, to the genteel house of ill-repute which did its briskest trade in Assembly week – brisker even than during the Edinburgh Festival, when more and more gentlemen preferred boys.

Before one Assembly the BBC sent me to Danube Street to ask the proprietor, Mrs Dora Noyce, if she was taking on extra staff for the big week. A young woman of heart-stopping beauty came to the door. "I'm from the BBC," I stammered. Judging by her expression she might have heard that one before. "I'm sorry, dear," she said sweetly, "but madam's resting. She's not seeing anyone this afternoon." If only I had been wearing a dog collar.

In the Assembly Hall itself there were few women, of heart-stopping beauty or otherwise. A producer asked if I would recruit among the commissioners a young(ish) woman minister for some studio panel. I scanned pew after pew of black suits and silver hair for someone – anyone – who would pass as a young(ish) woman until, in the back row, I spotted a possible candidate. I passed a message beckoning her to stardom – in so far as anything produced by the religious department could be called stardom. She was a goodish TV performer, and we might have used her again had she not run off with the session clerk a month later.

Although the Assembly was unrepresentative of sex (overwhelmingly male), age (late middle to geriatric) and class (upper-working to aristo), it was surprisingly liberal on questions of politics and morality. However it did have an unpleasant weakness for putting people in the dock. It cherished its right to act as an ecclesiastical court, deferred to lawyers (Kemp Davidson, its procurator and a figure of gravitas, was never listened to with less than complete respect) and exercised clerical discipline in a suspiciously vigorous manner at times. While frowning on sexual misdemeanour – the minister who ran off with the session clerk was regarded as beyond the pale – it happily issued practising certificates to a convicted murderer and an embezzler.

It had a further weakness – for addendums, deliverances, addendums anent deliverances, blue books, orders of the day, the whole bewigged paraphernalia of a dying church in which the substance had ceased to matter but the form lingered on. Outside, in the Edinburgh of Aids babies and heroin pushers, the capital of the dispossessed, few knew or cared what the Church of Scotland stood for: it had long ago ceased to be part of people's daily lives. The Assembly "meant well" – just about the most condescending thing you could say about anyone or anything – but it resembled not so much a national forum ("the nearest thing to a Scottish parliament", I lied shamelessly in my studio intro) as an asylum with TV cameras. Not for nothing did they call it "the playpen", that area within which the high heid yins were enclosed – the clerks in all their Judgement Day smugness. To the right of the playpen, on a bench reserved for past mods, sat the old men of the Kirk, energy spent. Above luxuriated the Lord High, a moustacheod wonder with a treble-barrelled title and a colonial past, or (more recently) a business tycoon in the drinks trade. And below him, the honest men of the parishes in their Sunday best, when they sang unaccompanied each morning the stirring psalms of their childhood, uttered a majestic sound resonant of former certainties. But was anyone out there listening any longer?

And yet, if only as pageant and symbol, the Assembly held some residual significance, especially in a country lacking a voice of its own. It was at least as worthy of attention as the Scottish Liberal Party conference attended by 79 community workers in some Highland hotel or the meaningless whingeing of the STUC comrades, both of which commanded a greater share of BBC Scotland's outside broadcast time. For several years, Assembly coverage was confined to a 10-minute "round-up" tacked on to the end of Reporting Scotland supplemented by extended coverage of the Church and Nation debate with its political focus.

Plainly this was inadequate, the more so since – if only the viewers had known – the programme was presented, not from Edinburgh, but from Studio B in Glasgow. Apart from a morning away for the interview with the new moderator, I spent the entire week in a dingy cubicle in Queen Margaret Drive watching a feed of the proceedings from the Assembly Hall and selecting, with Malcolm Coupar's help, a few morsels for teatime. Either it had not occurred to our masters that a reporter did his best work when he was allowed to attend the event he was supposed to be reporting – or it had occurred to them and they were indifferent. (Probably the latter.) Anyway, the Kirk was not best pleased with its treatment, and made its displeasure felt.

But when the BBC responded by upping its coverage and sending me to Edinburgh for the week, lo and behold – the Kirk still wasn't satisfied. I used to cringe behind the camera as the temperature rose; perspiring brows were mopped with order papers and rolled-up copies of the Scotsman, and bolshier commissioners pointedly took to wearing sun specs. True, the Assembly Hall did become fairly hot fairly quickly if the BBC pressed its full battery of lights into service: but was this not a modest price to pay for the BBC's hours of faithful devotion? Some of the brethren clearly thought not.

A point would be reached during each Assembly when one sensed that open season was about to be declared on the BBC. It was usually after lunch on the second or third day, by which stage the thermometer had reached sauna consistency and had taken its toll of Christian patience.

At this point, invariably during some drearisome debate, a purple-shirted clot in a creased suit would clump up to the podium, tweak his little beard, and address the chair in that weird declamatory style patented by the clergy. "Moderator," he would thunder, "on a point of order is it not possible for our friends (sarcastic emphasis) from the BBC (spat out like a dirty word) to do *something* (underlined) about these lights of theirs (rumble of agreement) before some of us pass out on the spot? (Much stamping of feet.) Moderator...(in case the man in the crazy gear needs to be reminded of who he is), I have heard (pained smile) of debates generating more heat than light (ho, ho: joke!), but perhaps (appeal to reason coming up) the BBC might consider the welfare of older (pensioner vote) commissioners."

It was an easy way to score a point: no skill required. Short of standing the cameras down and leaving a blank where the Assembly report should have been, there was not a great deal we could do about it. Everyone knew that: it was just the Kirk's way of reminding us that we were present on sufferance and that "the welfare of older commissioners" was considered of greater importance than a rare opportunity to evangelise Scotland through the mass media.

One year, Malcolm Coupar had returned to the studio to prepare the programme and I was the BBC's only senior representative in the hall when the complaint came. The speaker was from the far right of the fundamentalist fringe, those disturbed people who profess to believe every every word of the Bible, and as he left the playpen with the manic expression common to his kind, I decided that the Church of Scotland should be taught a lesson: though not necessarily from the Book of Proverbs.

I alerted the crew, and waited until a suitable moment presented itself. I didn't have to wait long. Another of the "fundies" leapt to the rostrum. We would let him have it. I gave a signal, and within five seconds plunged the Assembly Hall into darkness.

Not complete darkness, of course. The dimmish hall lights were still on – but the BBC blondes had gone on strike and without them it was as if instant midnight had descended. There were gasps and giggles from the body of the kirk and even a few of the past mods stirred from their half-life. Our theatrical coup had the desired effect of ruining the rant. Better still, it made a point about the BBC's integrity – we were here not as disciples of the Church of Scotland, adjuncts of its public relations committee, but as professional broadcasters in a country which, despite the annual rigmarole on the Mound, was rapidly becoming post-Christian.

The Kirk operated a fairly sophisticated PR set up, published its own magazine, ran its own theatre, and organised video training courses advising ministers how to look and sound good on the telly (I discovered that I was a poor teacher). Yet, when it really mattered, its communication skills were woeful. Unlike opportunistic political parties which timed their main conference debates to suit prime-time television, the Church of Scotland remained obstinately opposed to any accommodation with the BBC. Even when the Assembly was televised live, as it was for a few years in the early Eighties, the business managers resisted modest adjustments to the order of business which would have brought the vital business of Christ's kingdom into Scottish homes. On the contrary, they usually managed to ensure that the Assembly was at its most balls-aching just as the cameras went live.

"Don't tell me they're moving to the Chaplains' report," I groaned from the commentary box 30 seconds to on-air.

"Looks like it, I'm afraid," confirmed a rueful Ralph Smith, our OB director, himself a Church of Scotland minister. And if it was not chaps with medals being assured by the mod what splendid gung-ho fellows they were, it was some matron from the Woman's Guild summing-up another year of tattie scones and home-made jam or the convener of "Artistic Questions" discoursing at length on new approaches to stained-glass windows. "This is the nuts and bolts of Assembly business," I observed diplomatically in my best further education fashion. "Later in the day (tradespeak for 'When you lucky sods are watching the racing from Kempton Park'), there'll be a big debate on abortion." What I should have added was: "But needless to say, the chumps have so arranged things that we'll be off the air long before then."

One year, I entered the final morning's transmission with a hangover and could think of nothing to say. For what seemed an eternity – and in broadcasting terms 15 minutes is an eternity – I let the discussion unfold without commentary. I half-expected my colleagues in the O.B. van to rouse me, but no one did. Perhaps they thought I had died and gone to Hell. "Well," I said finally, "this debate on ministers' car allowances continues, but that's all we have time for. From all of us here at the General Assembly, good morning."

And on came Jackanory, bang on cue.

10

Department of miracles

"But, Ian, do you really believe in God?"

BBC Scotland's head of religious broadcasting paused, smiled one of his enigmatic smiles, and replied softly: "It depends what you mean." His challenger, a producer on loan from Light Entertainment, looked frankly horrified by Ian Mackenzie's ambiguity: clearly she regarded him as a heretic unfit to hold a powerful position in the Scottish Christian hierarchy. (People from Light Entertainment appreciate more than most the need for certainties in this life. It must take real conviction to produce the Hogmanay show.)

She was not alone. Many people of influence mistrusted Mackenzie and were convinced that he was out to destroy the Kirk. This opinion was commonly held not only among the bureaucrats and committee servers at Kirk HQ, but by decent, charitable men of independent mind. One of the most popular communicators in the Kirk, James Currie of Dunlop and Arran, shook his head in sad disbelief that I was working for Mackenzie. "Look at what he is doing," Jimmy muttered. "Of course I'm not welcome at the BBC any more."

It troubled me that there was bad blood between them – Scotland has too few good men that two of the best should quarrel. But, if my sympathies in this long-running feud lay anywhere, they lay with Mackenzie. From the moment he left the parish ministry to take up Ronnie Falconer's old job at Queen Margaret Drive, there was not the smallest doubt that he would challenge the staid orthodoxy of religious broadcasting. And that could only be healthy.

Unlike the woman from L.E., I never questioned Ian Mackenzie about his religious beliefs, but I suspect that he saw failure as the spiritual centre of Christianity. In his perplexed, sceptical way, he personified something that Iain Crichton Smith once said to me in a radio interview: "Scots are bursting with the courage of their own convictions, but what we need is to have the courage of our own doubts for a change." Mackenzie did have the courage of his own doubts. "It depends what you mean." Perhaps what he was really saying was: "It depends what *I* mean." Was this so very different from the question haunting the troubled souls of men and women in the closing decades of this crematorium century, in which the possibility of a loving God had been mocked by our knowledge of the gas chambers?

People looked in vain to the pulpit for help in resolving their confusion. Either the pulpit wasn't there any more – ritually sacrificed at the altar of "Unions and Readjustments" – or else it was occupied by some guitar-strumming fool with his New English Bible of Sunday Times prose and his unshakeable faith in the salvationist power of Morning Has Broken. Yet Scotland is a small country where basic questions of belief have merited the liveliest and most serious discussion. The existence of God is at least as respectable a topic for a Saturday night pub argument as league reconstruction. But one place where you will not find these questions debated vigorously is from the average Church of Scotland pulpit, with its strategic view of a sea of empty pews and a clock that stopped in 1953.

So BBC Scotland's new head of religious broadcasting made two assumptions which were eminently sensible. First he assumed – in so far as the established church would allow him to assume – that institutionalised religion in Scotland was moribund. Next he assumed a residual interest in Christian belief and precepts among the non-church-attending population and decided to address his programmes to that sympathetic though uncommitted majority.

By BBC Scotland's ca'-canny standards, this was extraordinarily bold. If Mackenzie meant business, logic dictated that he should dismantle traditional forms of broadcast worship which the church regarded as its right and had jealously protected in the face of small and dwindling audiences. Televised morning services, for example, would have to go – an unthinkable betrayal in the minds of many in the church. For this Mackenzie was never forgiven, least of all by his embittered predecessor, Falconer.

In place of the department's clerical-grey image, a more vital identity emerged. Of course I am biased here: quite often I was Mackenzie's studio man. But I take no credit for the flow of original ideas which emerged from this least likely of sources. For several years religion was the department where risks were taken. The Church of Scotland, which should have delighted in a higher profile, fumed. Privately, so did other BBC departments. For Mackenzie did news better than News, current affairs better than Current Affairs, light entertainment better than Light Enterainment. He stole everyone else's clothes and showed how to wear them with panache.

He possessed a gift which counts above all others in a creative business – he had an eye for quirky talent. Two of his most inspired appointments were also the strangest. He brought into his circle a Jehovah's Witness, Paul Streather, and the self-avowed "last of the Christian Marxists", Donald N. Macdonald. Not many BBC managers would have risked hiring either of these exotic creatures; it required exceptional intuition to have hired both.

I got to know Donald well. Paul Streather I knew hardly at all. He was a pale, withdrawn figure, a closed book emotionally, whose past remained a blank although there were hints of some profound unhappiness. A few months before his death in a car accident we met in a Glasgow street and he greeted me as he might have greeted a casual acquaintance before moving quickly on. We had worked on dozens of programmes – in Alastair Hetherington's opinion "these two together were very effective" – yet I have no memory of ever sharing a confidence or a joke or even having a serious conversation with Paul. A cold fish, I would have said. Yet his documentary films in which he encouraged people to talk about their lives were poignant and memorable.

In my first TV series for the religious department, I was with the formidable team of Ian Mackenzie (producer), Paul Streather (director) and Donald Macdonald (co-presenter). The series was called Eighth Day and went out live after the teatime news on Sunday. No one seems to remember it. Scarcely surprising, for it lasted only eight weeks and, inexplicably, was not brought back for a second run. Yet Eighth Day is one of the few programmes I made which still please me.

Studio-bound on a low budget, it set out to explore the ethical dimension of current events. Each week Mackenzie penned a stylish essay evaluating the news from a broadly moral or spiritual standpoint, but it was Macdonald's review of the week's press which made the stronger impression. Sharp, witty and provocative, Donald combined the mysticism of the Gael with the street-wisdom of a political radical: he was like no other minister I have ever met. Marooned at desks miles apart in the semi-darkness of Studio A in Glasgow, we encouraged each other across the chasm and developed an instinctive rapport. But even from our first meeting Donald worried me. He smoked constantly, and his nails were bitten to the quick. He looked and sounded like a man who lived too much on the edge.

As the only professional journalist in the small group which assembled in the Glasgow canteen every Sunday for a pre-programme briefing, I derived a certain amount of mischievous satisfaction from playing the hack. On the first Sunday I pointed out that a group of normally law-abiding citizens were proposing a campaign of civil disobedience in protest at some bureaucratic iniquity (I have forgotten what). They were meeting that afternoon. Shouldn't we invite one of them into the studio for an interview about the ethics of their action? Mackenzie, to my astonishment, agreed on the spot. We scooped the newsroom that night, as we did on several other occasions.

Whatever his failings, Mackenzie could not be accused of an interventionist management style. At no time did he attempt to influence the content of a studio discussion. As far as I know, Donald also enjoyed complete freedom within the laws of slander (which were always a factor when D.N. was around). Having selected his people Mackenzie let them get on with it. In that sense, he was the best department head I worked for at the BBC.

I was sorry when he chose not to develop the Eighth Day concept of applying news and current affairs skills to religious broadcasting. But his next project was more daring still – an audience participation series, The Yes, No, Don't Know Show, in which 50 people selected at random argued the toss on some issue of topical interest. Programmes of this kind are commonplace now, even something of a broadcasting cliché; but in 1976 the studio free-for-all, with the presenter moving in and out of the audience, was extremely rare; indeed I had not seen such a programme before I chaired one myself. In pioneering spirit, we made up the rules as we went along. We decided that the main rule should be that there were no rules. Rather than the usual tight-arsed structure familiar from a thousand current affairs setpieces, we would aim for anarchy.

But would it work? Since the format was untried, we could not be sure. We wanted to capture the spontaneous flavour of a pub argument, but Studio A was not remotely like a pub and the budget didn't stretch to getting the panel drunk in advance. I wondered whether a Scottish audience, mostly of people who had not been taught to articulate verbally, would clam up or be fatally polite to each other. A former principal of Glasgow School of Drama told me that Scottish students were so inhibited in their first few weeks that he used pantomime techniques to break down their reserve. Unskilled in such methods, I had 15 minutes in which to warm up 50 people unknown to each other and create the conditions for lively debate.

A few hours before the first recording, it began to snow heavily. Even in winter, the authorities are surprised by snow and ill-prepared for it. Road conditions in and around Glasgow quickly became chaotic, and the police issued their usual nanny-like warning to motorists to consider whether their journey was strictly necessary. By 6.30 – half an hour before the audience had been asked to attend – the city was silent. Most people had gone home early and there were few cars still on the roads. I scanned the list of invitees and was dismayed to note that many lived outside Glasgow. "We'll be lucky if anybody shows up," I said gloomily to Ian Mackenzie. "Yes," he said in that dreamy way of his. ("It depends what you mean.")

It is possible that the head of religious broadcasting had a word with the supreme controller of the universe and of all the road-gritters which crunch within it. Anyway, a small miracle occurred that evening. Most of the invited audience appeared and the few who didn't were replaced by conscripted reserves. Everyone had a horror story about the conditions "out there", and before long the studio was a babble of animated chatter: we could not have done a better job of re-creating saloon bar fellowship if we had recruited Bet Lynch of the Rovers' Return. The programme burst into life from the moment it went on air, and by the end Ian Mackenzie was beaming. Never had snow fallen more fortuitously. Never, alas, was it to fall for us again.

The show was deliberately – some would say shamefully – populist and teetered on the brink of bad taste. A proposition was put. The audience voted yes, no, or don't know. A discussion followed. At the end of the programme, the audience voted on the same proposition a second time. When this outrageous gimmick was first proposed, I made the banal observation that no one of any intelligence would change his mind about an important question of personal belief or morality on the basis of a TV discussion. I was wrong. We managed to sway opinion even on such matters as "Was Jesus God?" This was embarrassing. Yet, although the programme offended purist instincts, it stimulated and provoked. And, more valuably, it gave ordinary Scots a voice on television which, until then, they had been denied.

Needless to say the religious establishment was not amused. Ian Mackenzie protected us from our critics and, with the Scottish controller's support, bore the brunt of the attack. But it was only when I read Hetherington's memoir that I realised how rough the going must have been: "These programmes were shock-horror to some of BBC Scotland's Religious Advisory Committee. They objected first that some people taking part were not Christians and had said blasphemous things, second that the Christian religion was not always winning the votes, and third that it was chaotic, not intellectually sound."

True, all true – yet depressingly blinkered. The suggestion that religious programmes should only include Christians betrayed a bigoted view not only of broadcasting's public responsibilities but of the rights of other religions in an increasingly multi-cultural society; and the insistence that the Christian religion should always "win" the vote (what were they suggesting? that we rig the ballot?) confirmed everything I had ever suspected about the frightened little men who rule Christ's kingdom in Scotland. As for the complaint that the programmes were "not intellectually sound", I plead guilty and offer only one plea in mitigation: The Yes, No, Don't Know Show attracted one of the largest audiences achieved by a Scottish religious series and, for a while, became a talking point in grubby little pubs, on the tops of buses, and in all sorts of other places seldom visited by members of the Religious

The Closing Headlines

Advisory Committee.

Meanwhile, Donald N. Macdonald had joined Ian Mackenzie's staff of radio producers along with another rising young star of the Scottish ministry, Stewart Lamont. Macdonald and Lamont had little in common except an idiosyncratic outlook and a vigorous prose style. Both were entertaining company.

Donald asked me to be his jobbing reporter/presenter on an innovatory series, Crossfire, for the BBC's new "national network", Radio Scotland, which was as uncertain then about its identity and purpose as it is now, 15 years later. Crossfire, he explained, would tackle challenging subjects avoided by most religious programmes in the past – and it would tackle them head on. That sounded promising, although I had heard some of it before. Investigative journalism of any kind is notoriously expensive, and Donald's budget was minimal. But, like his boss Mackenzie, he hired well. Carolyn McAdam, who had been our vote-counter on the Yes, No, Don't Know Show, was recruited as research assistant, and a tenacious one she turned out to be. (She is now a director of an advertising agency, and that is the BBC's loss.)

The son of a North Uist crofter of anti-clerical views, Donald Macdonald had left home to attend school in Portree, where an eccentric English teacher, "Long Will" Robertson, instilled his love for words. Somewhere along the line he also acquired a liking for political disputation. He was a star debater at Glasgow University and entered journalism with the Beaverbrook papers in Glasgow, as so many young firebrands had done before him. Sent to report a Billy Graham rally in Glasgow, he surprised himself by being converted on the spot. From then until his death 37 years later, he combined political radicalism with theological conservatism: a potent island brew.

As minister at Partick, a working-class parish in Glasgow, Donald was at his best. He took the Gospel to the poor, the dispossessed, prisoners, the people with whom the Church of Scotland, in its complacency, had lost touch. He was, by all accounts, a pastor of exceptional gifts. Then he decided to become a full-time broadcaster. It was a mistake. He hated the bureaucracy of the BBC. Didn't we all? But Donald coped with it less philosophically than most. There was a baffling element of self-destructiveness in his temperament which went well beyond natural rebellion. He was combustible.

I liked him enormously. In the darker Celtic side of his character, his intense need for creativity, his anti-Establishment instincts and his paranoiac tendencies perhaps I saw a more dramatic mirror image of myself or what I might become. Of course I didn't altogether trust him. But then I didn't trust myself either.

BBC Scotland's schedulers, with their usual genius for doing the wrong thing at the wrong time, relegated Crossfire to an early evening backwater between two specialist music programmes, and the publicity department did nothing to promote it in Radio Times or the Scottish press. But Donald, in addition to his many other talents, had a penchant for self-promotion. He was sure that we would soon be generating our own publicity. And, very quickly, we were.

Living up to his promise to deliver outspoken treatment of taboo subjects, he announced an investigation into religious discrimination at Rangers Football Club. When he told me about the project, I groaned inwardly. Few journalists worthy of the name had not, at some stage in their career, attempted to do a spot of dirt-digging at Ibrox Park. Much good had it done any of them. Rangers' refusal to sign Catholic players remained a blot on the conscience of Scotland as it had always been. What more was there to say about it? But Donald was not to be discouraged. He persuaded the club's chaplain, my friend James Currie, to defend the obviously indefensible and pitched him against the bright young socialist journalist, Brian Wilson. This made for riveting listening. But Donald's coup was still to come.

"I want you to interview Willie Waddell." (The dyspeptic Waddell being the Rangers manager of the time.)

"Impossible," I said. "He'll never agree."

In Donald's case miracles did not take a little longer; they could be achieved pretty well immediately. I would simply ring the manager at his work and record a conversation with him; I would, however, refrain from telling him that we were recording it. We would, in effect, bug the manager.

I said to Donald that I wasn't sure about the legality of all this, but that ethically it was quite wrong and would almost certainly

The Closing Headlines

land us in trouble. He smiled winningly and said something about ends justifying means. OK, Waddell wouldn't co-operate, but he might let slip some revealing remark in a call which he believed to be off-the-record. Was I, so to speak, game? I was. But when? On the strategic side of lunch, he thought.

When Waddell came on the line I sat alone – never more alone – in a studio in Queen Margaret Drive with producer and engineer safely ensconced on the other side of the glass.

I explained that I was "doing some research" and would welcome his thoughts. He was incredibly abusive, and if the call had been broadcast, it would have been highly revealing of the manager's backwoods mentality. But about five minutes into the tirade, Waddell paused, drew breath, and declared in his belligerent tone: "Wait a minute. Ye're...ye're...ye're bluidy well recording this, aren't ye?" (Alastair Ford, drama critic of the Greenock Telegraph, was thus proved wrong: I was no good as a radio actor.)

Donald made a gesture signalling that I should tough it out. But my heart was no longer in this electronic subterfuge.

"Yes, I am," I owned up feebly.

"I'll hiv ye," he ranted. "I'll give this tae the papers, I'll file an official complaint to yer management. Ye hear me?"

Willie Waddell was as good as his word. Next morning the Scottish Daily Express led its front page with a juicy new scandal at the BBC – how the manager of Rangers Football Club had had a private conversation recorded without his knowledge or authority. There were grovelling apologies from "on high", promises that the offending tape would be destroyed, and unflattering references to Macdonald and Roy. It looked bad for us – I mean, seriously career-bad. But when I met the bold Donald, he told me not to worry. Either we were to put our faith in the Lord, or he knew something I didn't.

Verily another small miracle occurred. Or, rather, two small miracles. One was a rave notice by Kathleen Rantell in the Glasgow Herald ("shines like a gem...on the level of top rank productions on Radio 4") and the other was a rave notice by Harry Reid in the Scotsman ("the flagship of Radio Scotland"). Willie Waddell had done us a favour: he had put Crossfire on the map.

11

David Niven changes his shirt

Between 1972 and 1978, when I worked for the BBC full-time, I must have averaged five interviews a week – which, allowing for holidays and other absences, amounted to a hot-air total of 1,440. Who were all these people? And what on earth were they on about?

Even now, strangers stop me in the street occasionally. "You once interviewed me for the BBC. Remember?" I rarely do. But it says something about the skewed nature of modern mass communications that they should still remember me, the passive conduit of their opinions and expertise. So I ask myself: out of 1,440 interviews, how many can I call to mind? And the answer is: precious few. Either the subject matter was so inconsequential that it was spat out almost before it was digested; or the interviewees were too dull to leave a permanent impression. Often it was a bit of both.

Richard Dimbleby claimed towards the end of his life that at the centre of broadcasting there is a hollow. He didn't say what causes it, but I will hazard a guess: it has to do with the ephemeral nature of the medium. Even the daily paper which some use to wrap fish suppers is preserved by others on microfilm for future study. But the radio or television interview dies the moment it is born. "In one ear, out the other" – who would want that for an epitaph? Yet it is carved on every broadcaster's tombstone.

Of the interviews I do remember, most are discoloured snapshots of a particular mood or moment, curiously selective in their focus, often disconnected to the spoken word. Of Nigel Tranter, the novelist, I remember only his purposeful stride along Gullane sands one damp autumn morning. I remember a Piskie bishop with a name like hare soup only because he accused me of

The Closing Headlines

asking a tendentious question – but of the question itself, or its answer, nothing. I remember an interview with that fine Tory MP, Alick Buchanan-Smith, only because we shared a taxi along Princes Street after it.

Some people I remember for their names. Munn, Dunning and Pack were industrious dominies who conducted, simultaneously, three long-running inquiries into Scottish schools. Which was which? Their faces, their reports, their public pronouncements, so familiar and important at the time, now dissolve into amorphous anonymity. I wonder whether their work accomplished anything or whether educational standards continued to slide regardless. At least I can picture Dr Christopher Clayson's kindly face. He was the other great committee man of the 1970s, the begetter of Scotland's more "civilised" drinking laws (also known as grotty all-day pubs).

Others I remember because they evoke a sound. The bark of Eric Heffer, the socialist MP, on a radio link from London – what a disagreeable fellow he turned out to be; or the accountant's drone of Bruce Millan, Labour's last Secretary of State for Scotland; or — never to be forgotten — the snarl of Willie Waddell...

And there is one I remember with pangs of guilt. An Edinburgh man, an adventurer, advertised his intention to sail round the world in a flimsy boat and I interviewed him for radio the day before his departure. At the end I wished him well but added some ill-chosen words to the effect that he should not expect to come back alive. It was meant as a joke, but sounded heartless and tactless. As it happened, the poor man failed to return from the voyage and was presumed lost at sea. Later, a newspaper reported that he (or his ghost) had been "sighted" in his native Portobello.

Then there were interviews memorable for their embarrassment. Worst by far in this category was a botched job with my mentor, the journalist James Drawbell. He had retired with Sheila – his partner? wife? I never knew – to a flat overlooking the sea at North Berwick and a radio producer, aware of our friendship, expressed an interest in an "in-depth" conversation piece. I asked Jimmy if he would prefer to record the interview in the Edinburgh studio, but he wouldn't hear of it. Margaret and I must come for afternoon tea to North Berwick, and we would have our little chat there.

He was his usual jovial self during the social preliminaries, but as soon as the women left the room and I switched on the Uher, his demeanour changed. He became edgy; even mistrustful. What did I propose to ask him? How much ground did I propose to cover? I gave the answer I always gave – that there was nothing which destroyed the flow and spontaneity of an interview more quickly than an agreed list of questions. Couldn't we just see how it went? Warily he agreed.

Jimmy, who had been raised in abject poverty in Falkirk, his home town and mine, emigrated as a young man and worked briefly in Canada before crossing into the United States. In New York – the city of Scott Fitzgerald, who befriended him in a bar – he knocked on door after door until he persuaded a newspaper to hire him. He returned home and conquered London. By the age of 26 he was Fleet Street's youngest editor. Even in the incurably romantic trade of journalism, there were few stories to match the rise of young Jimmy Drawbell. It should have made a compelling radio programme.

"Let's begin," I said chirpily, "with your first impressions of New York. Now, when would that be?"

He put his hand over the microphone.

"No, no," he protested. "We mustn't mention dates."

"Why not?"

"The dates don't matter. In fact, I'd rather we didn't talk about America at all."

I put the recorder aside, and he explained what I knew already – that he had entered the United States illegally. I might have said: "So what? It's half a century ago. Do you seriously think they're going to get you for it?" He had, in any case, been quite candid about his American experiences in his autobiography. What had got into him? But because he was a friend and an old man, I let it drop. Shaken, I confirmed that nothing would be said about America.

I tried a different tack, but that didn't work either. The interview stumbled from one monosyllabic answer to another, and Jimmy's pained expression made it plain that I was asking all the wrong questions. "Look," he said, "I think we'd better pull the plug on this, don't you?" I nodded: I had little choice.

Although the rest of the afternoon passed awkwardly, the

The Closing Headlines

incident did no lasting damage and I overlooked a curious sequel a few months later when I heard him give a long radio interview in which he spoke warmly of his time in America. A marvellous man – but a mysterious and capricious one. His obdurate attitude might even have been a way of punishing me for deserting the printed word in favour of broadcasting, which he regarded as the needless squandering of a promising talent. Who knows? Jimmy is long dead.

The Drawbell interview was probably the only one of significance that I had to abort. But I came close with my rudest subject, that wayward son of socialism, Lord George Brown.

A notorious drunk of disfigured political gifts, Brown was down but not quite out when he accepted a sleeping partnership in some Edinburgh consultancy business. Wrongly, the appointment was judged newsworthy enough for a short interview on Reporting Scotland, which I suspected he would use as an opportunity for a blatant puff. It was to be my last interview of a hectic day, but the filming fell behind schedule. I rang Brown's office and explained to his secretary that we would be 15 minutes late. Not to worry, she trilled; the good Lord would be around for the rest of the afternoon.

When we arrived, 15 minutes had turned to 20 and Lord George was counting every second. Behind an empty executive desk sat the former Foreign Secretary in self-righteous fury. He was, as they say in Glasgow, roarin' fu. Roarin', anyway. "What the bloody hell time do you think this is?"

Bob Werrilow, the Edinburgh cameraman, one of the best and nicest in the business, grunted into his beard.

"We rang to apologise..." I stammered.

"Never mind bloody apologies. So this is the way the BBC in Scotland treats people, is it? Bloody nerve you people have. Sheer bloody arrogance. Turn up when you bloody well like, and expect other people to jump. Well, some of us have better things to bloody well do than hang around for the BBC. That clear?"

We got our interview. And George Brown, such a bully off-camera, became sweet reason for the duration of his free ad.

It is a disappointing fact that most politicians in their private dealings with the media are just as you would expect. Lord George duly behaved badly. Neil Kinnock talked about – what else? –

The Closing Headlines

Welsh rugby in the studio warm-up. Denis Healey introduced himself to the BBC's Edinburgh doorman, Bob Laing, as Mike Yarwood, his impersonator. Willie Ross ("old Basso Profundo") acted to perfection the part of the disciplinarian headmaster. But the one who in my experience was truest to his caricature was Roy Jenkins, our star guest in a political programme.

"Better make sure," said Tom Ross, the producer, "that we have a decent claret waiting for him."

"You are joking, of course."

"Not at all. Can't have the usual cheap plonk."

Surely, I thought, the excellent Thomas was going too far and Jenkins's reputation as one of the great wine connoisseurs of the modern era must be exaggerated. But, all right: we would see. After an interview which he would have called "agreeable", Jenkins joined us in the hospitality room and Tom produced his decent claret. Very decent indeed, judging by the price. The last hope of British social democracy pronounced himself well satisfied with our discriminating choice, before lecturing us elegantly on matters of the day.

"How much of Roy's claret passed your lips?" Tom asked later.

"Didn't get a look in," I replied truthfully.

"Nor I," he beamed.

Even the dullest politicians were more fun than the generality of stage and screen actors, those vacuous personalities of the telly chatshow circuit, few of whom had anything to say for themselves beyond the heavy plug for their latest product. An exception – the only one I remember – was David Niven, who breezed into Edinburgh to publicise his latest volume of autobiography. Unlike most stars, Niven arrived unaccompanied by the usual retinue of hangers-on. He brought just himself and a battered hold-all.

Donald Monro with elaborate courtesy settled him into the studio and left for the gallery. I was taken immediately by Niven's modesty, warmth, and intelligence – an attractive combination in any man but almost unheard-of in a Hollywood great. And then he threw me with a request unique in 1,440 interviews.

"Would you mind," he said, "if I took off my shirt? It feels a bit sticky."

"Sure. Go ahead."

Donald was less sure. Into my earpiece came the sound of the news editor's familiar sardonic laugh followed by the message: "Ask him if he's proposing to do the interview naked from the waist up. Should probably let Glasgow know."

For a few moments it did indeed seem that David Niven was contemplating a striptease. Off came the sticky pink shirt, revealing a bronzed body.

"Sixty seconds," intoned a voice from afar.

With perfect timing, the master produced from the battered hold-all a crisp, freshly laundered shirt, changed on the spot, and replaced his beautiful silk tie.

"That's better," he said – and we went straight into a funny, delightful interview.

Now that's what I call class.

Of Scots who could be called great, I interviewed only two. (Perhaps there were not many more.) Both, alas, were well past their best. I stayed in the same Iona hotel as Lord MacLeod of Fuinary during some theological convention and was struck by his bearing, marvellously erect for a man in his mid-eighties. His voice, too, was strong, still with that prophet's ring which had captured the open hearts of the Scottish church if not the closed minds.

Indeed there didn't seem to be much physically wrong with the octogenarian George MacLeod aside from the fact – awkward when it came to interviewing him – that he was as deaf as a post. "What's that?" he would roar, one hand cupped to his ear, the other gripping his crook. What I wanted to ask was why the Iona Community, rebuilt by the unemployed craftsmen of Govan in the name of a just society, had been allowed to become a retreat for limp sandal-wearers, the shriller feminists, and counsellors in meditation. But that would have struck too churlish a note, even if he had heard the question.

Like MacLeod, Hugh MacDiarmid lived to a grand old age. I spotted somewhere that his 85th birthday was approaching and, on the assumption that he wouldn't celebrate many more, hastened to Brownsbank, his tiny cottage near Biggar, to compile a birthday

The author as he was in 1973. It looks like a suit – but it isn't

A BBC news film crew in action. Bob Warrilow is the cameraman. 1973.

Perils of celebrity (1). K.R. crowning a gala queen circa 1977.

Perils of celebrity (2). Was it something he said?

annual ritual...interviewing the Mod in the shadow of
Knox's statue. David Steel in 1974.

Patrons and friends...Left: Finlay J Macdonald. Below right: Donald N Macdonald. Bottom: Ian Mackenzie Opposite: Jameson Clark as the policeman in Whisky Galore

The West Sound team...including front row: Allan Andrews (second from left); Sandy Webster (fourth from left); Bryce Curdy (fifth from left); Lou Grant

Sandy Webster in his pre-West Sound days as a tabloid tyrant. Note the frozen smile!

Tommy Truesdale, an Ayrshire man whose heart lies in Memphis, Tennessee.

The author as he is today.

tribute for Reporting Scotland.

I realised on the way there that I was terrified of meeting MacDiarmid. He had a well-deserved reputation as one of the fiercest curmudgeons in the land. He was known as a heavyweight drinker who went 15 rounds to the bell. In short, he was the stuff of demonology. But I did my homework and prepared the questions with more than usual care.

The birthday boy came to the door to greet us, a literary lion framed in the doorway of a doll's house. I gazed in wonder at our benevolent host, so warm and welcoming, and tried with difficulty to match him to the vituperative figure who nursed some of the longest grudges in modern literature. Others who knew him better have remarked on the contradiction between the public and private faces of MacDiarmid, one as vengeful as the other was compassionate. I would not have believed it had I not experienced it for myself. I can only say that he was one of the sweetest people.

The same, unfortunately, cannot be said of Valda, his second wife, a formidable Cornishwoman with a shrewish tongue, who played – or so it seemed to this unfamiliar visitor – the domestic dictator to MacDiarmid's hen-pecked husband. Or perhaps she was simply being fiercely protective and had seen too many freeloaders and main-chancers at Brownsbank for her to be unduly impressed by fresh trouble. Anyway, she gave us a cool reception.

All went comparatively well, however, until MacDiarmid tentatively proposed that the guests should be offered a wee refreshment. Valda blew up. *"There will be no drink,"* she commanded, and one half expected her to fetch a rolling pin from her tiny kitchen. It was a statement curiously reminiscent of Jimmy Reid's "Nae bevy" order to the shipyard workers of the Upper Clyde, and with the same impressive result. MacDiarmid accepted her word without dissent, winked knowingly to the crew, and the critical moment passed. There was no drink – not even a soft one made from girders.

The poet sat eagerly in an old armchair by a coal fire and spoke with some passion about the events and people of his long life. Although he would have talked for hours, we only had 10 minutes. But I recorded more than Reporting Scotland could ever have used, knowing that I would find a market for the extra material when the time was right. As it happened, this was MacDiarmid's last television interview: he died the following year. Crossfire had started by then, and I suggested to Donald Macdonald that we should do a programme about the representation of Scotland in its poetry and fiction. "I could offer you an exclusive interview with Hugh MacDiarmid," I added casually. "You could?" said Donald. "Hmmm. Never before broadcast." We milked it for all it was worth – which was quite a lot.

And there, I fear, my limited fund of interview anecdotes runs out. Whatever happened to all those others who consumed the greater part of my working life for so long? Did anything they say change anything? Can I remember a sentence – even a word – that they told me? No. All gone. "Down the tube". That is the essential character of television. That is the size of the hollow.

12

Limbo

Several of the journalists I knew in the 1960s were non-motorists, but the weaker succumbed eventually. Ian Jack, when we met in London after his appointment as editor of the Independent on Sunday, apologised for driving me to lunch. However, William Hunter still goes everywhere by public transport – indeed one of his finest hours in journalism was an account of a bus journey to Bonkle – and, although I believe Stuart Trotter has a full licence, the political correspondent of the Herald never uses it. As for me, I am a confirmed non-motorist in the way that other men are confirmed bachelors. I place driving in the same category as snorkelling, incest, holidays in Tenerife, and ballroom dancing, all of which I am content to leave to others.

I was the only non-motorist in the Glasgow newsroom of the BBC, but people were tolerant of the disability and no one ever complained that it affected my work. When it was practicable I went by train; if not, one of the crew gave me a lift. This had the additional benefit of saving the cost-conscious BBC mileage expenses.

But then, unexpectedly, I hit a problem. Disenchanted by short-term contracts and longing for security – how I had changed since the rebellious days of long hair and frayed denims – I applied to be BBC Scotland's first staff reporter, which would have entitled me to a pension and other perks. I was "boarded" (interviewed) and got the job. There was only one caveat lurking in the small print: staff reporters must possess a current driving licence.

A man called Peter Donnelly, the personnel officer, was insistent: there could be no exceptions to this rule. But, he added soothingly, the BBC would be willing to pay for lessons and I would be allowed six months in which to pass the test. Despite these concessions, I returned unhappily to the newsroom and consulted Ross Anderson. The head of news dismissed the matter as a minor inconvenience and with my usual eagerness to postpone evil days, I promptly put it out of mind. Peter Donnelly, however, did not forget; to BBC bureaucrats, the small print in offers is the beginning and end of the known world. When the six months were up, he demanded to see me in his office.

"What about those driving lessons?"

"I haven't taken any," I admitted. "I've decided that I don't want to drive. I've always got on OK without a car."

"That's not the point," Donnelly replied quietly. "It's a condition of the job. You accepted our offer on that basis."

"I know, and I'm sorry. If it's absolutely non-negotiable, you'd better appoint someone else."

"Very well."

"Does that mean I'm back to being a contract reporter, then?"

"I don't know. We filled your original post. There are no vacancies at the moment."

"What are you saying? That I'm fired?"

"Could be," he said with a shrug.

I never saw Donnelly again (he took the high road to London – by fast car, I hope) and Ross Anderson gave me general reassurances which stopped ominously short of a guarantee. So I entered a kind of limbo. The contract which had expired when I became – or didn't become – a staff reporter was never renewed. Strictly speaking I suppose I had ceased to exist: I was a non-person. But, this being the BBC, my former employer continued to pay my former salary into the bank at the end of every month. Nothing had changed, except that I was more vulnerable than ever. There could be no long-term future in it.

Margaret kept a diary throughout 1978, a BBC diary which allocated a page to each day. I felt unwell for most of the first half of that year, although the ailments were largely psychosomatic in origin and a direct result of my growing unhappiness at work. I came to dread the dreary underground to Kelvinbridge, the trudge along Great Western Road with its Indian restaurants and oriental grocers – to this day the smell of curry reminds me sickeningly of the BBC – and the heart-sinking turn into Queen Margaret Drive. More than anything I dreaded the false bonhomie of the newsroom with its middle-aged men in shirtsleeves. This was not Dimbleby's hollow. It was something deeper: a void.

The sense of insecurity was so corrosive that I could scarcely bear to see anyone else present Reporting Scotland on "my" weeks for fear that the new pair of shoes, once under the desk, would not be easily budged. In June I made an indecently early exit from a family funeral so as not to miss the programme. Two years earlier I had presented it even on the day of my father's funeral, offering the excuse that work would "take my mind off things". Both times I was motivated by paranoia – the occupational hazard of the television anchorman.

But there is some truth in the sour modern proverb that anyone who is not paranoid is not in full possession of the facts. George Sinclair and his henchman, Bob Millar, descended on me with the idea – nothing definite, you understand, just something to ponder over the summer – that I should cease to present the programme and concentrate on the longer films "which you do so well".

"In that case, who would present the programme?"

"Malcolm Wilson," George replied rather too quickly.

Going back on the road full-time, particularly if they allowed me a free hand, would have at least one attraction: I wouldn't be imprisoned in the Glasgow newsroom every other week. But removal from an up-front role was certain to be interpreted as that familiar BBC ploy: demotion dressed up as an exciting new challenge. I said I would think about it. George smiled one of his indulgent fatherly smiles and repeated that, really, there was no urgency.

If he felt that it was "time for a change" – the most feared words in broadcasting – I could hardly complain. In an industry which thrives on permanent revolution, I had survived six years in the hot seat. As Alastair Hetherington put it in his book, I deserved a long-service medal. Instead I had an overdraft and a fractious bank manager, a mortgage three months in arrears, and no prospect of advancement. In desperation or for the hell of it – there wasn't much difference – I applied for a producer's job and was turned down because I was too valuable to the BBC as a "performer".

One consolation during this bleak period was my membership of an old, companionable Glasgow club of academics and hacks.

The Thirteen, who met on or around the 13th of the month for dinner and argument, included Jack House, gentle doyen of Scottish journalism, and David Baxter, editor of the Scottish Community Drama Association's magazine. David dropped a hint that, at the age of eighty-something, he was thinking of retiring. I said without hesitation that I would like his job; I more or less pleaded for it. Although, at £250 per quarterly issue, it was not the highest-paid editorship in the land, it gave me a creative energy which years at the BBC had sapped. But it was not enough. It was a distraction, not a solution.

On June 30 1978, my old friend, the fiendish flasher of Breakish, left the BBC to run his own video production company. As I stood at the back of the newsroom watching the presentation of a parting gift to Malcolm Coupar, my mood grew blacker with every joke, every secretarial giggle, every billow of Bob Millar's pipe. Contemplating the absurdity of this scene with its insincere conviviality and heartiness, it occurred to me that I must give up or crack up.

That weekend we began our annual family holiday in Nethy Bridge, a pretty village in Inverness-shire, where we rented a cottage with a burn at the bottom of the garden. Nethy in my memory is a place of heat, raw Speyside whisky, Wimbledon on a dodgy black and white telly, afternoon tea with the Misses Cheyne and Morrice, 24-handicap golf, and long walks through an ancient pine forest. But this was not one of the better Nethy years. Margaret's diary records that I had a cold for much of the fortnight. I felt little better when we returned and stayed off work for a few extra days.

On July 24, I prepared to face the Kelvinbridge underground. I got as far as the garden gate of our douce semi-detached in Prestwick before turning back.

The doctor diagnosed "debility", a euphemism for a minor nervous breakdown, and I went to bed for a week, slept a lot, and in conscious moments vowed never to return to the newsroom. George Sinclair was reluctant to accept my wife's protestations. He said I must rest; take as much time as I needed; and – an unexpected gesture which made me feel worse – the BBC would go on paying me until I was feeling better. Unknown to him, the decision had been made. George offered more money – £3,000 a year more – which would have eased our financial problems. I had no difficulty in resisting.

It would not be exaggerating my dread of the Glasgow newsroom to call it a physical revulsion, although I wonder whether I would have felt the same about any open-plan room. The forcing together of people of dissimilar character and temperament into such workspaces is anti-human: an invasion of the basic need for privacy and peace. But perhaps the dread went deeper. In the lavatory at the end of the corridor I had seen a nice man, Jim Herd, one of the newsdesk executives, popping pills to control his blood pressure; a year or two later he was dead. I could think of several causes worth risking my life for, but dying to bring Mr and Mrs McFlannel the six o'clock news from Airdrie Sheriff Court had never been one of them.

We sold the Prestwick house and leased a draughty 16th-century castle 15 miles to the south, at Maybole. Its best feature was the splendid turreted exterior on which Charles Rennie Mackintosh based his design of the Glasgow School of Art, but inside the property had been messed about by the Victorians and the central heating which spluttered up from the dungeons via a boiler nicknamed Vesuvius was not only ineffective but ruinously expensive. Yet the living, though primitive, was stylish. Indeed the hairy-jumpered existence of an Ayrshire laird might have suited me if I could have afforded it. But George Sinclair's generosity and patience finally ran out, and plans to set myself up as the last of the gentlemen publishers got no further than a small paperback about golf and a smaller one about the theatre, each of which sold about 300 copies and just about paid the printer.

In the absence of anything else to fill the gaps between boozy sessions in the Star Inn, our side-street howf behind the Castle, I drifted back to the BBC on a more casual basis. Ross Anderson, who had been moved to Edinburgh, asked me to present a new lunchtime slot on radio and there were occasional stints of Good Morning Scotland with Jack Regan and others. But, so disillusioned and exhausted had Reporting Scotland left me, the only programmes I enjoyed making were Donald Macdonald's features – not because they were well-paid (they paid horribly) but because of their subversive content.

One programme we did together, on an alleged conspiracy at

Carstairs state institution for the criminally insane, was so outspoken that the BBC refused to broadcast it. For a long time Donald believed that our lives might be in danger as a result of the trouble we had stirred, but I was less concerned about the risk of being murdered by a mad axeman from Carstairs than by the thought that Donald's Hebridean imagination had finally got the better of him.

With Donald I made my first visit to the Outer Hebrides and discovered the darker springs of that imagination. He had sold to Radio Scotland the idea of an interview series, Faces of Uist, in which older inhabitants of his native island would talk about their customs and beliefs. But I suspected that his long-suffering senior producer, Douglas Aitken, had mistakenly understood that he (Donald) would be conducting the interviews. When Donald rang the office and let slip that "Kenneth is with me", I detected some surprise at the other end. "Will my air fare be refunded?" I asked anxiously. "Don't worry," he laughed, "we'll work something out." Typical Donald.

At Benbecula, where I was shocked by the incongruous obscenity of the rocket range and the overbearing military presence, we hired a car which bumped over a causeway into the peaty moorland of North Uist. Finally we arrived at the scattered village of Lochmaddy and booked into the only hotel.

The owner waved us upstairs and invited us to select any rooms we fancied. I paused at the top of the stairs and, instead of following Donald and his assistant Carolyn McAdam along the corridor, climbed a few further steps to an obscure room detached from the rest. I peeped inside. It was plain and a bit gloomy, with heavy furniture and a chipped wash-hand basin. But it was clean. It would do. I unpacked and joined the others in the bar. Later I did the first of the interviews with a retired district nurse, a cheery, practical woman, who described the "little people" – fairies – who lived in the neighbourhood as she might have described one of her patient's corns.

Tired and uneasy, I went to bed late, couldn't sleep, and was gradually convinced that that there was someone else in the room. I sat upright and – I can put it no other way – tried to "face the presence out". I was aware that the visitor was sitting at the foot of the bed. But there was no ghost-like shape; nothing whatever to be seen. It was "only" a feeling. After a while, the oppressive atmosphere lightened and I fell into a dreamless sleep.

Over breakfast I told Donald what had happened. He looked curious, but said very little. In the afternoon, during a break from the interviews, we drove miles to the majestic Atlantic coast where he had grown up. Donald stopped the car at a spot soaked in melancholy. There was a precipitous drop to the sea. Leaving him by the car, I scrambled down so far that, when I turned to look, he was reduced to a tiny figure on a distant horizon. I thought: the sea looks inviting, I will walk into this friendly sea, I will be carried away by it. Then Donald's voice – a shout from above – pulled me back.

Afterwards I said: "Wasn't it odd, the sheep fank (pen) at that place we stopped the car? I've never seen such a thing before – the model sheep leading all the others in."

"I saw no sheep fank."

"You must have seen it."

"No," Donald said emphatically.

In the bar that night, the proprietor was not surprised to hear of the presence in my room. There had been similar reports. In the 1930s, a Roman Catholic priest had slit his throat in this room, staggered into the corridor, and died in the adjoining bathroom – as good a case for en-suite facilities as any I have heard. The proprietor said that the bloodstains had resisted all attempts to remove them; look carefully on the bathroom floor and you could still trace a faint mark. Well, this was a fine way to scare the tourists.

(Twelve years later, I visited the Lochmaddy Hotel a second time – alone. I checked in and was shown to the same room as before. It had been modernised and seemed larger. Then it dawned on me – they had knocked down the wall between it and the notorious bathroom. I slept without incident.)

The other and, to my mind, more intriguing mystery seemed to irk Donald. We drank and talked through the night, and the more we drank and talked, the more insistent he was that there had been no sheep fank. In the end he became quite agitated and demanded that we should return to the spot forthwith. "Don't be so bloody stupid," I said. "It's four o'clock in the morning and we're pissed. Want to get us killed, do you?" Instead we wandered out into a cold dawn. The village shop was already open – it never officially closed – and Donald bought cigarettes. We returned to the bar and cleared up, the barman having retired at a reasonable hour. Later that morning we flew home. He never mentioned the phantom fank again, and when I reminded him of it years later he claimed to have no memory of the incident.

I made my own inquiries. A friend at the Scottish Agriculture Department said that the sheep I had seen – or thought I had seen – was known as a "Judas sheep": they were fairly common. But had there been a fank? He asked me to pinpoint the spot on a map and said that he would consult the agricultural records of North Uist. A few days later he rang with his answer. "So far as I can tell," he said, "there haven't been sheep in that precise part of the island for about 100 years. But I could be wrong."

I am still perplexed by this experience for which, of course, there is a possible rational explanation: my friend from the Scottish Agriculture Department did get it wrong, the sheep fank was there all the time, Donald was having me on. Later, however, I learned (and had confirmed from a second source) that where I felt the compulsion to walk into the sea a party of nuns once drowned. Is it possible that, for a few minutes, I experienced an overwhelming sense of the unhappiness of that place – perhaps even imagined the scene, not as it was now, but as it had been? I could have settled the matter. I could have gone back. But I didn't go back. I never will.

In July 1993 Donald rang.

"How does it feel to be Douglas Aitken?"

"What do you mean?"

"They've repeated extracts from Faces of Uist on Radio Scotland and credited Douglas as producer/presenter."

I couldn't tell whether Donald was amused or hurt or both. He was proud of Faces of Uist and regarded the series as a personal testament. But right to the end it was a curiously ill-starred venture. I did not hear from him again. A week later he was dead.

Two surprising things happened in the final weeks of 1978, the year I quit Reporting Scotland. First, I was asked to make the annual Children in Need appeal for the BBC's charity – a strange request considering that I had recently left the corporation's full-time payroll. My sons Stephen (aged 10) and Christopher (seven), presented the programme with me and we raised a decent amount.

And then, in the final days of that peculiar year, Ian Mackenzie said in his usual laconic fashion: "I've just heard. Alastair Hetherington has been fired."

"What?"

"Yes, he's going to Inverness as station manager. When I rang Elizabeth [Ian's wife] to tell her, she thought at first that he must be joining British Rail."

He was not. At his own suggestion he was joining Radio Highland, a BBC version of Siberia.

Although Scottish aspirations had not been officially buried yet – the referendum was still three months away – the events of 1978 finished Scotland for a generation. Hetherington's defeat after an exhausting three-year battle against the BBC's centralised power symbolised a wider and greater defeat. Public opinion, particularly in the Highlands and Borders, was turning against an Assembly; the SNP's "first 11" had made fools of themselves by voting with the Tories and against the Lib-Lab pact – a treason for which the party was to pay dearly; and, silly as it sounds, the humiliation of the Scottish football team ("Ally's Army") in the World Cup in Argentina caused general despondency. Scotland had managed a draw with Iran; what really hurt was that the one Scottish goal had been scored by an Iranian player. Before long, we would be world experts in own goals.

BBC Scotland was a duller place without Alastair Hetherington. Working there lost much of its point: he had not handled London adroitly, but he represented the hope of a future which was slipping from our hands. Meanwhile, Donald Macdonald, who might have built a broadcasting career on the strength of all those glittering notices, had given his self-destruct button another push and left to join the Iona Community (from there it was downhill all the way). Suddenly the people I was working for were play-safers, non-rock-the-boaters, straight-down-the-middlers – the people with whom London could deal and had been used to dealing. We had flirted with risk, but the effort had been too much. Alastair Hetherington and the others who re-invested in Scotland might just as well have stayed away for all the difference it made in the end. How comfortably we reverted to our dependence culture.

In this depressing climate, politically as well as personally, I came to a decision that I should abandon broadcasting and devote myself to the Scottish Community Drama Association. The SCDA's full-time director was on the point of leaving and I felt pretty confident that, if I wanted the job, I could have it. The idea was immensely appealing. It paid a regular salary, it was a cause worth fighting for, and it would enable me to see more of Scotland. Not least, I would be free of the BBC at last. But I didn't become director of the SCDA. Instead I got another of those random telephone calls which, in the absence of any grand plan, dictated what passed for a career.

13

How to refuse £50,000

The proprietor of our local bookshop, Keith MacDonald, a Labour councillor in Ayr, rang to suggest that we should start a radio station. I might have laughed.

"This bloke's been on the phone," I said to my wife. "He wants me to start a radio station."

"Why not?" Margaret replied.

We stoked Vesuvius in honour of Keith MacDonald's visit to the Castle just after New Year, 1980. He told me that the Independent Broadcasting Authority – IBA as it will henceforth be known – was proposing to advertise a franchise for commercial radio in Ayrshire. Now, let's get this right. Not commercial (sordid word), but *independent* local radio – ILR as it will henceforth be known.

I knew vaguely about the plan, having read bits and pieces in the local press, but it had not interested me until now. I had never listened to any of these pop and prattle stations, but noted from the papers that the programmes were named after the presenters and that it paid to be called Gary, Mike or Kenny if you wanted an upfront job in local radio. Well, I suppose I was a Kenny...up to a point.

"Any ideas on programmes?" Keith asked.

"Oh, lots of news," I said grandly. "As much interesting local stuff as possible."

The councillor nodded sagely.

As the discussion unfolded, there seemed to be two practical problems in our way. First, the franchises were put out to competitive tender and Keith was convinced that the Ayrshire prize would attract several bids. Second, even if we won, we would need a great deal of money – perhaps as much as half a million pounds – in order to put Gary, Mike and Kenny on the air.

We speculated nonchalantly about possible sources of finance and agreed that the money should be raised locally. Keith envisaged no great difficulty, but emphasised the need for a well-balanced consortium including a token woman, a token trade union organiser, a token arty-fart, a token educationalist, as well as the usual brigade of hard-faced chaps with the loot. But, this being a branch of public service broadcasting, even the financiers might have to be of passable character. Ideally our consortium should consist of filthy rich Kirk elders. I told Keith that he could put me down for £2,500.

First things first: an exploratory meeting with "interested parties" in a room of the Savoy Park Hotel, Ayr. He would contact a few, I would contact a few, and we would see if anybody turned up. In the event, there were not many refusals. Among the great and the good of Ayrshire who appeared were R.D. Hunter, a music buff and former town clerk of Cumnock, who was always bow-tied but never tongue-tied; Craig Brown, a college lecturer, manager of Clyde Football Club in his spare time, poor man; William McIlvanney, Kilmarnock's best-known novelist; Robin Knox-Johnston, a round-the-world yachtsman who had put down anchor in Troon; and a senior manager of Scottish & Universal Newspapers (S.U.N.), proprietors of local papers in Ayrshire and elsewhere.

Although Keith chaired the meeting skilfully, the atmosphere was subdued. In an attempt to brighten things up, I said provocatively that ILR stations were too preoccupied by trashy pop music. The fitba' man kicked me off the park for this elitist observation and pointed out that they were in business to make money. "If all we're proposing is a radio station no different from the rest of the crap," McIlvanney responded, "I don't know why I'm here." In that crisp exchange of polar opposites, the essential dilemma of ILR – how to reconcile commercial imperatives with programme quality – was laid bare. I doubted whether it would be happily resolved.

The newspaper manager, silent for most of the evening, piped up with a realistic refrain. His firm would be interested in backing a consortium with a "business-like" approach, but we should be under no illusions: applying for a local radio franchise was likely to be a bruising affair. I took this as a rebuke for my airy-fairy notions of a station dominated by intelligent talk.

After the meeting, I had a look at my diary for February and March – one drama festival after another as well as BBC commitments – and concluded that I didn't have the time to help Keith MacDonald further. Of course I could have made time. But, although I liked him, I didn't approve of politicians running local radio stations. They ran practically everything else – why give them the freedom of the air as well? I was unhappy, too, about the possible involvement of a media conglomerate which already controlled many of Ayrshire's weekly papers. The suggestion that S.U.N.'s monopoly of local opinion should be extended to part-ownership of a radio station struck me as unhealthy. Keith, on the other hand, believed that local radio would benefit from their expertise and that, in any case, we couldn't afford to spurn them. No other potential backers of any substance had emerged; maybe none would.

Before I set off to adjudicate the season's drama festivals, I dropped him a note, formally withdrawing and explaining why. Surely I had heard the first and last of local radio.

Not quite. James Ballantine, an old Beaverbrook hack of excitable temperament, rang to find out what I knew. He disclosed that two senior men at Radio Clyde were helping him to form a powerful group in Irvine New Town, where he was PRO of the Development Corporation. He didn't ask for help and I didn't offer any.

It was a rather less confident James Ballantine who rang in late February. Radio Clyde's men had withdrawn. There were dark hints that James Gordon, the station's wily managing director, had discovered what was afoot and dissuaded his employees. Whatever the explanation, Jimmy had been let down. How would I feel about helping him out? I half-heartedly agreed to chair a meeting in Irvine on condition that any consortium should be representative of Ayrshire as a whole and not just of the new town. Jimmy's main concern – he was quite open about it – was to ensure that the radio station came to Irvine rather than Ayr or Kilmarnock. I didn't necessarily disagree. Location was the least of our problems at this tentative stage.

The meeting in Irvine Burns Club was depressing and poorly

111

attended. The sole source of possible financial support, a Kilmarnock industrialist, sat glumly at the back of the room and muttered something at the end about reserving his position. But Jimmy remained unputdownable. Next he dragged me to Glasgow for a chat with Derek Webster, chairman of the Scottish Daily Record.

Webster, who occupied an executive suite of deep luxury, poured three fine malts and got straight to the point. The Record had just backed the new radio station in Dundee, where the managing director was a clever young man called Allan Mackenzie. Now the Record would like to support the Ayrshire station. Another clever young man, Liam Kane, would be seconded from Record House to assist us. Jimmy Ballantine nodded enthusiastically at this point, I somewhat less so.

"How much, then?" Derek Webster asked. "How much is required?"

"Well," I replied slowly. "I don't know. How much would you say?"

"We would be talking £50,000."

"I see," I said. "Well, I'll think about it."

It was in the taxi to the station that I realised that no one had ever offered me £50,000 before and that, like a fool, I had said I would go away and think about it. Jimmy was at once exultant and baffled – exultant that, with Webster's support, his Irvine consortium seemed doomed to success; baffled that I could not share his joy. But there was an issue of principle at stake here and, though not clear cut, it was worth defending. At a heavy pinch, S.U.N. might be acceptable as major shareholders in the radio station; at least they owned papers in the area. But a line should certainly be drawn before the involvement of a national newspaper group with no interest in Ayrshire other than a narrowly commercial one. Indeed I was rapidly coming to the view that if the people of Ayrshire could not or would not back a radio station with their own money, they didn't deserve to have one. I tried to explain these fastidious distinctions to Jimmy Ballantine, but without much success. We parted company.

Although I was getting nowhere fast, I had developed a mild taste for the local radio idea. I thought I might even have a go at setting up my own consortium. Yet, without firm backing, there was no point in further meetings of local worthies. What I needed was one blue-chip local business with some spare cash for a speculative investment. Then, anything would be possible.

One morning in March, I was on a train to Edinburgh when I spotted a brief report in the Scotsman: the IBA was formally inviting applications for the Ayr franchise and had set May 28 as the closing date. This was a tighter schedule than anybody had anticipated. From a cold start, it left two and a half months in which to form a consortium, raise promises of the cash, and prepare the application. The task seemed pretty well impossible. But with the Irvine initiative crumbling and rumours of other embryo groups failing to materialise, Keith MacDonald and his newspaper friends apparently had a clear run. The moment had arrived when I must put up or shut up.

I hurried to Queen Street, made short work of a radio programme, and spent the rest of the morning hunting for possible leads. A press release pinned to the newsroom wall listed the CBI's Scottish Council members and among the names was one William B. Miller of Prestwick Circuits, Ayr. I had not heard of him, but was intrigued to discover that we were near-neighbours in Maybole.

A few evenings later, when I went to see him at his house, I was determined that a refusal would be conclusive. I had wasted enough time; this must be the end of the road. Miller was quiet, curious and shrewd, a clever businessman who had established an international electronics company employing several hundred people. Gently he teased out my views on the value of local radio to the community and offered some opinions of his own on the technical aspects of the operation. Then we turned to the nitty-gritty. How viable was the enterprise? Did it promise a return on investment? How quickly would it move into profit? Avoiding bullshit, I replied that the proposed station was one of the smallest in the IBA's network, that it would have a struggle to establish itself, that I could not visualise it as a licence to print money. Far from sounding discouraged, Bill Miller seemed to welcome this blunt appraisal of the situation.

A few days later, he rang to tell me that his company would pledge £25,000.

Buoyed by the news, I booked a room at Prestwick Airport for another meeting – only this time I could promise the participants some action. Most of my original contacts had joined Keith's consortium, but R.D. Hunter was still waiting in the wings and responded positively to a second overture. Iain Foulds, rector of Irvine Royal Academy, and Paddy Harris, organiser of the Scottish air show, were with me too, along with Bill Manson, a research chemist at the Hannah Research Institute, who had been recommended as a well-liked local figure with good contacts in the farming community.

On March 21, take-off day at Prestwick Airport, Ayrshire had its heaviest snowfall for years; but, after my experience with the Yes, No, Don't Know Snow, I regarded chaos as a lucky charm. Sure enough, we had a full house and the makings of a consortium. We decided to go out with the begging bowls. We were official.

"If you fancy running your very own radio station," wrote Archie Venters in the Ayrshire Post, "then you must have a look at the specification document produced by the Independent Broadcasting Authority. You'll find that it's not a case of nipping round to the nearest ex-Army shop and picking up a couple of old service transmitters. There's a lot more to it than that."

How true. The IBA's exam paper included questions on "applicants' capacity to run a lively and distinctive radio station", "relevance of the suggested programming to the locality", "realism of the plans and their likely capacity to stand up to the tests of time" and "financial soundness of the proposals". I calculated that if we were to answer all 41 questions properly we would require to write the equivalent of a decent-sized novel, hope that the plot didn't creak, and pray that our characters were plausible.

As a reward for passing the exam, the IBA charged the successful applicant £28,500 a year. Bill Miller's cheque wouldn't even pay the rent for the first 12 months.

Eric Dale, our man in Irvine, went the rounds of his friends and produced a long list of supporters who were prepared to stump up the minimum investment of £1,250. Others did likewise, though not so persuasively. R.D. Hunter, who had been installed as chairman, was making headway with the Royal Bank of Scotland. But we were still a long way off target. The S.U.N. executive – he of the businesslike approach – called to say that he had lost confidence in Keith's consortium and wished to join ours. Panicked by the continuing shortfall, I agreed that he should attend the next meeting.

It was a bad mistake. No sooner had the meeting begun than he insisted on making a statement. Word had reached him that it was no longer a two-horse race for the franchise. A dark horse had entered, and it was none other than Radio Clyde.

This unexpected news was not well received. How dare they! The sheer nerve of it! Quickly I consulted the IBA's spec with its emphasis on "significant elements of local ownership and knowledge" and "the local nature of the services to be provided". How could a Glasgow-based company fulfil the spirit of these requirements? Yet our informant was insistent. Not only did Clyde intend to apply; it was his opinion that they stood an excellent chance of winning.

Jimmy Ballantine, whom I had invited because I felt sorry for him, made matters worse with a speech knee-deep in conspiracy theories. Clyde meant business, he assured us in his two-packets-a-day voice. The station's management was actively touting for Ayrshire support. Approaches had been made to un-named "prominent people". He had heard that James Gordon was preparing to meet Keith MacDonald's group to establish whether there was room for compromise – perhaps even a joint approach to the IBA. This revelation was greeted with angry cries of "Sell out". The suspicion in the room that Ballantine himself must be a party to the treachery was palpable. But still he ploughed on, digging an ever-deeper hole for himself. Clyde, he confided, was also eager to meet members of our group – collectively if possible but (the killer touch) *individually* if necessary. The implication was clear: we should expect some move to pick off our key people.

There was a second shock on that turbulent evening in the Station Hotel, Ayr, when I realised that I had been misled by the newspaper company. It had not withdrawn from Keith's group: far from it. Rather it wished to be part of both groups; it was everybody's friend. But ("naturally") it would respect the confidentiality of the rival groups' discussions.

The company's man pretended to be perplexed by the uproar which followed. MacDonald knew that he had a foot in both camps and had not objected; why should we take such a great huff? We were being hysterical: unprofessional: we simply didn't understand "the way these things are done". Our legal adviser, Robert Gardiner, a wise old bird, restored order by proposing formally that Scottish & Universal Newspapers should be expelled from the meeting and excluded from the group. The newspaper executive gathered his papers and left the room.

We were £25,000 poorer – £75,000 if we counted Derek Webster's unwanted cheque – and we were making powerful enemies. But we hadn't blinked. This was encouraging.

At the weekend, the Ayrshire Post confirmed Clyde's bid and quoted a spokesman for James Gordon: "The best service will be provided to the people of Ayrshire if the proposed station is regarded as an associate of Radio Clyde." And, just as Ballantine had predicted, our two rivals flirted with an engagement. Afterwards Keith MacDonald issued a statement: "Radio Clyde made it clear that they see the new station as wholly owned by Clyde and run on an opt-out basis for specialised Ayrshire programmes. I personally doubt if this will meet the IBA's criteria, which state that the new station should be owned and run locally, but that will be for the IBA to decide."

Surprise, surprise, there was no attempt to pick off our key people – only some half-hearted lobbying of the chairman. Either Clyde had got the message that we were incorruptible or James Gordon had decided that we were not serious contenders. The latter view was the one favoured by the local press, which had MacDonald and Gordon battling it out on the front pages with incidental references to "Kenneth Roy's Maybole consortium". I did nothing to improve our low profile; in fact I welcomed it. Maybole would play a quiet game.

In the end, we made our target of £250,000 ordinary share capital and could have exceeded it easily. Bill Miller spoke to somebody who spoke to somebody else who spoke ... and soon I was surrounded by whey-faced accountants and their clients, all anxious to be part of the great adventure. One of our new shareholders, when I referred to him loosely as a car salesman, corrected me sharply: "Call me a motor distributive agent". We had come a long way.

One evening at Prestwick Circuits, Bill Miller picked up a

pencil and casually drafted a list of the key staff posts. Over the words "managing director" he hesitated, gave me a quizzical look, and said in an expressionless tone: "I suppose that'll be you." It was not the most flattering job offer I had ever received. At the next meeting, I said that, having thought about my place in the scheme of things, I would prefer the job of programme director. There were few protests, and Miller again began doodling with his "staff structure". By the end of the night I had been positioned to the right of, but slightly below, the "managing and commercial director" (un-named) and the two jobs were connected by a row of ambiguous dots. As Ian Mackenzie might have said: "It depends what you mean."

On a Sunday evening in May, the weekend before the deadline, Bill Miller arranged to have his secretaries on hand to type up the application. By midnight I hadn't quite finished writing the masterpiece and the company secretary was sent out to fetch fish suppers. We wound up around 3am. Later that day, Bill Fyfe, one of the directors, flew to London with a bundle of 30 green folders for the attention of the IBA. On the front were typed the words: "Radio Ayrshire Limited. Application for the Ayr Local Radio Contract." We had made it with only hours to spare. But made it we had.

14

The prize

Before our first meeting with the IBA, I did a bit of digging in Who's Who and discovered that Britain's most powerful quango was ruled by a committee of academics, has-been politicians, and theologians. "Bloody typical," spluttered one of our captains of industry. "What do that lot know about running a business?" To which the obvious response was: "And what do you lot know about running a radio station?" From IBA headquarters we received a summons to attend for interview in the Station Hotel, Ayr, on June 24 at 11.50am. Few of my colleagues seemed overly concerned by the prospect; the general feeling was that we were dealing with a bunch of dilettantes, we'd show 'em, etc.

Out of the blue came a letter from Patrick Gallagher, a broadcasting consultant and former managing director of LBC (the London news station), offering his exclusive services for a modest – an almost suspiciously modest – fee. He suggested that groups preparing for an interview with the IBA were well advised to seek expert counsel; if I was in any doubt about this, I should call John Thompson, the IBA's director of radio. He might as well have suggested that I call God. But I was worried enough about the small-town arrogance of the businessmen in the group to hire Gallagher without delay.

He undertook to come to Ayr for a mock interview with the panel. But first he must read the application.

"It's not bad," he said when he rang a few days later. "Not at all bad. I've seen applications that were a lot worse. It's probably better than average."

"So you think we might be in with a shout?"

"I'll be tough for you. But you've given them something to think about."

Over dinner in Ayr he told a horror story which illustrated how easily the unwary could be trapped. A consortium somewhere in England had worked long and hard to prepare an application. Several very distinguished people were on the board. They were impeccably financed. The application had been well researched and beautifully written. Everything about this consortium seemed right. So how come they'd lost?

At the first interview with the IBA, the group's chairman was asked to elaborate on some aspect of the document. "Well," he replied cheerfully, "as it so happens, I've been pretty busy recently and haven't had the time to read the application thoroughly. But we have good chaps in the group who know all about it. May I pass you over to...?" They were not invited to London for a final interview. One careless remark had cost them the glittering prize.

"So we could be eliminated at the first hurdle?" I asked Gallagher.

"Oh, sure," he laughed. "The preliminary interview is probably more important as a test of a group's general capability."

With forensic skill, his voice rarely raised above a soft monotone, Patrick Gallagher proceeded to rip us apart. He seized on the weak points of the application and demolished them; worse, he made it appear that some of our people had a less than encyclopaedic knowledge of what was in the document. In an attempt to cover our tracks we were forced into damaging contradictions and non-sequiturs. Everybody talked at once. It was a shambles.

After a coffee break, he interrogated us a second time. We were a little better, though not much; at the end, Gallagher bravely forecast that we would "get it right on the night". In a private chat later, however, he told me plainly that our verbal presentation had been markedly weaker than the written application and that, making all allowances for nerves and the unfamiliarity of the experience, we might have a problem at the interview. "Remember," he said finally, "you've got less than an hour to sell yourselves."

Even the cockier entrepreneurs among us were chastened by the ordeal and realised that what lay ahead was a short trial followed in all probability by sudden death.

Before it met applicant groups, the IBA offered the public an opportunity to have its say. In most cases this was a token gesture to the consultative principle, but the unique circumstances of the Ayrshire franchise, with an established ILR contractor bidding to extend its territory, lent some weight to the public meeting in Ayr Town Hall on the evening of June 23.

Patrick Gallagher advised us to attend but to say nothing. Rival consortia grinding their axes in public the evening before the interviews did not earn brownie points from the IBA: no matter the provocation, he repeated firmly, we must not utter a word. About 150 attended – a respectable number for a hot summer's night. The IBA contingent led by Lord Thomson of Monifieth looked as grim as a funeral party when they climbed on stage, although Thomson did try a few tiny jokes about his political associations with Ayr before declaring the meeting open for the public's questions and comments.

The quality of the discussion was dire. Would the local radio station broadcast the results of the local flower show? Thomson, glancing at his watch, replied indulgently that he was sure it would. Another flourished a schedule of all the programmes he ("as an ordinary listener") would like to hear. Straining to keep my vow of silence I prayed that someone would address the critical question: did Ayrshire want its own radio service or was it content to be a satellite of Glasgow? In the nick of time, up jumped a North Ayrshire industrialist who confessed that he was an active supporter of Radio Clyde's application. Ah. This was promising.

"I think Clyde is best for the job," he said emphatically. "It is well-established and successful and is already serving around 45% of the people of Ayrshire." It was the familiar Clyde argument, but expressed with unusual vehemence.

James Gordon, who was seated in another part of the hall, did not look best pleased.

"Bill...Bill..." he hissed.

But his friend was in full flow and not to be stopped. "I want the new station to be successful," he continued. "But an independent station serving a population of 300,000 just wouldn't be viable. This area has suffered so many closures and redundancies, it has the smell of death about it."

It was a respectable case: no doubt about it. But it could be construed as a criticism of the IBA for advertising the franchise in the first place: no doubt about that, either. From the platform Professor John Ring declared with magisterial authority: "So far the IBA has not started an unsuccessful radio station, and we have no intention of starting one here. We are not mugs at this game." A young woman in the audience, Anne Myers, entered an impassioned appeal for a genuinely local radio station and insisted that the people of Ayrshire deserved no less. She was loudly applauded.

A few of us met for a post-mortem in a hotel obscure enough to avoid the embarrassment of bumping into Thomson and his chums. Instead we bumped into James Gordon and his chums. Some awkward banter was exchanged, and Gordon explained that he was hosting a dinner party for Clyde's "friends and associates" in Ayrshire. How fascinating. One wondered who they might be. The first to appear was the Kilmarnock industrialist who had "reserved his position" that dispiriting evening in Irvine Burns Club. But reserving it no longer.

Next morning Margaret and I arrived in the Station Hotel early enough to observe the comings and goings. Clyde's contingent showed first – a dark-suited trio led by James Gordon. Next in line was his chairman, the publisher Ian Chapman. But who was this bringing up the rear? The face seemed familiar. "Well, you'll know Sir Charles O'Halloran, of course," Gordon said, and Ayrshire's best known politician, the convener of Strathclyde Regional Council, grinned sheepishly. James Gordon had conjured out of the hat either a master stroke or a proper Charlie; I couldn't decide which.

By 11 o'clock, with 50 minutes to the off, we had been joined by Bill Manson, our technical consultant Jim Donaldson, and miscellaneous well-wishers. Nerves were shot to hell; the coffee flowed. The IBA's Glasgow officer, Veronica McDowall, came over to our table and exuded warmth; short of actually leading us by the hand she could not have given us a more positive reception. If only Veronica McDowall had been conducting the interview.

There were seven of us and, when we entered the room, it looked like hundreds of them. Among the sea of faces I spotted Thomson, the acerbic Ring, and the authority's Scottish member, Dr Bill Morris, minister of Glasgow Cathedral. John Thompson was there, too, maintaining the lowest of profiles. A shorthand writer took notes.

Lord Thomson, with the smile of a favourite uncle, said at the start that the meeting would be informal in style, far from the inquisition we might be expecting. From his wheelchair, R.D. Hunter beamed back. And I thought: Gallagher has warned us well. We would not be fooled by this softly-softly ploy. Well, not much. And Hunter, who was skilled at playing the part of the kenspeckle "Mr Ayrshire" figure, made an attractive opening bat. He managed to mention Robert Burns and Tar McAdam in the first minute.

I kept waiting for the googly.

"Why do you believe, faced with what will be fierce competition from an established station over quite a part of the area you will be serving, that you can make a go of it?" The question was Thomson's and he was no longer smiling.

"Competition from Radio Clyde is not a serious problem," replied our accountant.

Thomson retorted: "Are you speaking as a business man or as a local patriot?"

"As a business man who has put his name to the figures."

"Why is it not a problem?" asked Ring peremptorily. "It seems to me to be a very real problem."

We waffled round this, but generally it was turning into a creditable performance; Gallagher would not have been wholly dismayed. Our finest moment came when Ring suggested as an "unlikely contingency" a Radio Clyde investment in the company. Hunter demurred. "You could not see any advantage?" Ring persisted. "No," our chairman repeated confidently. "We can get any amount of money here." It was the right answer, and it was straight from the shoulder.

Bill Miller volunteered to deal with the last spot of bother. "Is there not some risk," Thomson suggested, "that if you got the franchise, Mr Roy having pretty well created the whole thing and getting the same salary as the managing director, you would not find people queuing up to be managing director?"

"The structure," Miller replied cryptically, "is based on the personalities we know today." And I thought: you had better do better than that in London.

By the end of the hour, I was satisfied that we had done enough to win a second interview, if not the franchise itself. My hunch was that the IBA would ask to see all three groups again. I was wrong: they unceremoniously dumped Keith MacDonald's consortium with its heavy dominance by newspaper interests (Webster's Daily Record having joined S.U.N. under the same umbrella). After making so much of the running in public, Keith and friends were reported to be shocked by their abrupt rejection. On the other hand, "Kenneth Roy's Maybole consortium" would be going to London. And so, of course, would James Gordon's Radio Clyde. A straight fight.

The grapevine was working overtime. I heard from reliable sources that, although we had impressed the authority with our spirited approach, Clyde would enter the home straight as 60-40 favourites. These were discouraging odds, but they were by no means hopeless. We could still swing it. The question was: how?

The key to the outcome was surely our handling of the Clyde question. I thought hard about it in the month leading up to London and put my conclusions on paper:

"We should grasp any opportunity to emphasise that the social characteristics of Ayrshire are very different from those of Glasgow and that our programming reflects the distinction. We would not attempt to create a duplicate of Clyde in Ayrshire for the simple reason that Ayrshire is not Glasgow. Clyde has 'captured the articulacy of Glasgow in a way BBC Scotland and the ITV companies have never managed to do...it has scooped Glasgow patter out of the street and got it on the air' (extract from Headlines: the media in Scotland, edited by David Hutchison). We should quote this and say that we share the author's perception of Clyde's success. In doing so we achieve two plusses at the same time. We are heard to be complimentary about the IBA's favourite station; and we associate Clyde with the Scotland of the big city. By contrast Ayrshire has a more clearly defined middle-class and highly-skilled working class, as well as a substantial rural population. Clyde, we say, has triumphantly identified with its area – an area remarkably homogeneous in character; our programming is designed to enable us to identify with ours – with its more subtle mix."

Vigorously argued, that might reduce the odds in Clyde's favour to, say, 55-45. But we were still lacking the X-factor: that extra bit of inspiration which would give us a fighting chance. For the life of me, I couldn't think of any.

Then R.D. Hunter rang.

"Seen this morning's Herald?"

"Yes..." I unfolded the newspaper on my desk. Perhaps there was something about the franchise.

"The opinion poll on the front page...see it?"

What was he on about?

"I see it. So what?"

"It's done by a firm called System Three. Ever heard of them?"

"Yup, they're a market research outfit in Edinburgh. They have a good reputation."

"Right!" When excited, as he often was, the chairman talked in exclamation marks. "Get on to them right away and commission an opinion poll! We'll show these IBA bastards that Ayrshire wants an *independent* local radio station! They won't take our word for it! But if this System Three could prove it, we'd be home and dry!"

It was an inspired idea: he would never have a better one. But what about the money?

"Damn the expense! I'm giving you my personal authority as chairman to go ahead!"

System Three said that, at a push, they could accomplish the fieldwork and analysis before we left for London. But the question would have to be put fairly if we were not to invite charges of bias. In the end we agreed to offer a choice between "a new, independent, locally-based radio company" and "an extension of Radio Clyde's present service to Ayrshire". We settled for a sample of 500 evenly weighted throughout the transmission area.

The outcome, though likely to go our way, was not beyond doubt and the timetable could not have been tighter: canvassing, July 19-20; results analysed, July 21; data completed, July 22; London, July 23. But the more I thought about it, the more I was convinced that System Three's poll, produced at the right psychological moment during the interview, would be a climax worthy of Terence Rattigan. Though only, of course, if we had a result worth producing.

The presentation folders were waiting for me at System Three. I had ordered one for each member of the IBA. Such hope. Such bravado. I grabbed the top copy and went straight to the only statistic that mattered: for a locally-based company: 66%; for Radio Clyde: 34%. Even among regular Clyde listeners we had won a decisive majority. And nowhere in Ayrshire was the vote against Clyde heavier than it was in Irvine New Town – where most of the people were native Glaswegians.

Bill Manson and I chose the slow way to London by train, while the others flew. We met in the Capital Hotel in Basil Street, round the corner from the IBA's Knightsbridge HQ, for a lunchtime snack of adrenalin, black coffee and G and Ts. The idea was that I should give the group a final pep talk. But there was little left to say. The man from S.U.N. had been right: it had been a bruising affair, and it wasn't over yet. But after four months we had earned the right, if not to win, at least to fail with honour.

Inside the IBA, we were escorted silently to a seventh floor anteroom and told to wait. Patrick Gallagher's last words were ringing in my ears: "You're on your own, young man. It's David v. Goliath." A door opened and Lady Plowden, chairman of the IBA, strode forward. "We're ready to see you now," she said briskly.

15

A clean sheet of paper

A month later John Thompson rang. It was my first direct contact with the IBA's director of radio. He wished to see us in Ayr, but we must understand the need for the strictest discretion. "I won't...actually...be there...if you get my point." A picture of Alec Guinness as master spy George Smiley came to mind. "Quite," I said. "I'll say nothing to the press." Nor, Thompson urged, to anyone else outside our board of directors.

We were to meet in a room of the Station Hotel on August 20. I suggested dinner afterwards. There was a long pause. "Ah...we'll see," he said in a distant tone.

Thompson's shifty call was the latest unsatisfactory move in our nerve-wracking negotiations with London. The final interview in Brompton Road turned on the incongruity of my position as No. 2 in the pecking order. At the end Plowden proposed bluntly to our chairman that I should be nominated as managing director. Hunter sort of agreed. By that stage we would have agreed to anything. We had begun to scent victory from the moment Plowden asked if we had any evidence that our plan for local radio was what the people of Ayrshire wanted, and I theatrically produced one of System Three's folders with the assurance that there were enough copies to go round.

Although we were bundled out the back door – an undignified exit which might have symbolised the IBA's evaluation of our chances – the interview went better than any of us had dared hope. There was nothing further to do but wait. So I took off with the family to a small hotel in Galloway and tried to forget local radio.

One night we were in the bar, recovering from a 14-mile walk to a remote railway station featured in Dorothy L. Sayers' detective novel Five Red Herrings, when I heard a telephone ringing in the manager's office next door.

"He's not here, I'm afraid. Can I take a message?"

Later the manager came into the bar. "Oh, I didn't know you were back. "You're to call a Dr Manson in Ayr as soon as possible. I've got his number."

The rest of the night passed in alcoholic euphoria. The IBA was "minded" to grant us the franchise. *Minded.* A cautious word – but surely enough to justify a toast or three. It was only when I returned home and studied the detail of Plowden's letter to R.D. Hunter that the euphoria started to evaporate. Most of the authority's qualifications and conditions could be satisfied, but there was one major difficulty: the insistence on a share issue of £400,000 rather than the original £250,000. Raising the extra money would be child's play, but it would inevitably dilute the shareholdings of the founders and directorships might have to be found for new backers. Bill Miller was cross about the size of even the present board (nine) and had told me that he was not used to having to deal with more than three people at a time. I could not foresee him capitulating to pressure.

It took me almost as long to prepare a report for the IBA dealing with dozens of minor points raised by Plowden as it had taken me to write the original application. With Jim Donaldson and a London architect who specialised in building radio studios, I began a tentative search for premises. Although we saw nothing remotely suitable, I was not concentrating very hard. Everyone around me assumed that the franchise was in the bag, but as the days passed and turned into weeks, Plowden's curious half-offer looked more insubstantial than ever. She had said she was "minded". But might she not exercise a lady's prerogative and change her mind?

Press speculation fed the growing atmosphere of unease and the suspicion that we were caught up in a plot thicker than a Dorothy L. Sayers thriller. A report in the Ayrshire Post that we had emerged as "clear favourites" was not what I wanted to hear. "Negotiations are still taking place between the IBA and both interested parties," said a Radio Clyde spokesman. Both? Either this was one of Dorothy's five red herrings, or the authority was playing silly buggers. Even more disturbing was a quote from the IBA itself. "To my knowledge," said an un-named spokesman, "we are still talking to both consortiums. A decision is not expected until September."

Despite my hunch that James Gordon was too skilled a political operator to be written off until the ink was dry on a contract, it was a cocky board of directors who gathered in the Station Hotel for the critical meeting with Thompson. Bill Fyfe, self-styled provider of "janitorial services", sped to Glasgow Airport to fetch the guest who wouldn't actually be there. Tactics were agreed: we would offer no more than a marginal concession to the IBA's demand for a hike in the ordinary share capital. I feared trouble.

Thompson arrived late. He eyed us warily, avoided social niceties, and got straight to the point. We were under-staffed and under-financed: what did we intend to do about it?

The staffing question was easily resolved. We caved in.

Next, the shares. We had under-estimated the difficulties of getting a radio station up and running. We had made no provision for foul trade winds. We were vulnerable. We needed a cushion. Any ideas? The tone was uncompromising. If we were serious about wanting the franchise, we would have to deal.

Someone feebly suggested an increase in the share capital from £250,000 to £275,000 – well short of the IBA's demand. There was no response from Thompson: not a flicker. How about £300,000? Still no good. The bidding would have to go higher. "Mr Thompson," Bill Fyfe squawked, "you've got to understand, all these extra ordinary shares will throw out our financial gearing completely."

"That is your opinion, I dare say," came the withering reply.

At 325,000 shares, Thompson called off the auction. Judging that he had pushed us as far as prudently possible, he said that the authority might be prepared to allow us to borrow the remaining £75,000; but we should be under no illusion – the IBA would require to see £400,000 on the table and not a penny less.

The director of radio joined us for dinner after all. The last supper might have been more cheerful. Bill Fyfe did his janitorial best to create a party mood by proposing a toast to the new radio station, but I noted that John Thompson raised his glass with something less than overwhelming enthusiasm.

"So – that's it, then," said Bill, determined to wring some commitment from our guest.

"W–e–l–l," Thompson responded. "Rather up to the authority, isn't it?"

All being well, the matter would be settled at a full meeting of the IBA on September 4. On September 5 I presented my last programme for the BBC and waited for word. September 6 was a Saturday – another blank. Then on Sunday Bill Fyfe phoned in a panic.

"Kenneth, I have terrible news. Just had the Glasgow Herald on. They're looking for a quote. We've lost the franchise. They've given it to Radio Clyde."

I was too shocked to say anything.

"Of course I told them I couldn't comment without speaking to you first. What should we do?"

"Let me think. I'll call you later."

It didn't add up. John Thompson, though he drove a hard bargain, had impressed me as a man of integrity. If Plowden had indeed exercised a lady's prerogative and decided at the last gasp to entrust Ayrshire radio to James Gordon's safe pair of hands, I felt pretty sure that the director of radio would have let me know before now. Could this be another cruel twist in the convoluted plot – another of those red herrings? Perhaps it hadn't been the Glasgow Herald newsdesk at all. Perhaps Bill Fyfe had been set up by a hoaxer and fallen for it. On the other hand...

The phone rang a second time. Bill again? The Glasgow Herald? Neither. This time, it was John Thompson from London. And, all defences down, I let him have it: "We're being pestered intolerably by the press. Our nerves are shredded and we can't hold out any longer. You must tell me whether we have won or lost the franchise." Still there was no definite answer. Could I be at the IBA offices no later than 11 next morning? I was to come alone.

On September 8 – eight months after the plot was hatched – the thriller finally reached its denouement. John Thompson, shirt-sleeved and relaxed, received me warmly. A press officer joined us and a statement was agreed. Radio Ayrshire Ltd. had been offered the franchise "subject to contract". So, to the end, the authority kept the door slightly ajar. We were expected to spend a quarter of a million pounds building offices, hiring staff, equipping studios, yet without the legal document which permitted us to broadcast.

I flew back to Scotland and hastily convened a victory press conference in the Station Hotel, Ayr, scene of so many of our dramas; as a nice final twist I booked the same room in which we had endured our first grilling by the IBA. It was a day of great excitement: there would not be another like it. "How do you feel?" a BBC reporter asked me. The honest answer would have been: "As high as a kite."

Bill Manson brought me back to earth. "Well," he said drily, "that's the easy bit over."

James Gordon was among the first to offer his congratulations. But he made it clear in his letter that the IBA had reached the wrong decision, and nothing would budge him on that score. He could not accept that a small station operating on the territorial edge of a much larger one was likely to be a viable proposition. I put that down to big-station thinking. He had never run a small station where the economies of scale were quite different. We were the corner shop to Gordon's supermarket. Although we couldn't afford Clyde-built dramas and documentaries, we should still be capable of providing a respectable service to our community. Gordon argued, however, that all radio stations irrespective of size faced inescapable overheads. In his view the sums made no sense. (He was proved wrong: 12 years later the Ayrshire station was still in business.)

Despite his misgivings, James Gordon wished me success. He imagined that I must be feeling as he had felt when Clyde was awarded the Glasgow franchise – deep satisfaction at the prospect of starting from scratch with a clean sheet of paper.

Later, when I met him at a conference of ILR chief executives he gave me some advice. "Enjoy yourself for the next year. Have fun while you're building the station. Once you're on air, if your experience is anything like mine, you'll spend all your time putting out fires." The metaphor puzzled me – I was to discover its truth soon enough – but I thanked him for his letter and said that its reference to a clean sheet of paper had caught my mood.

Though clean, the sheet was not entirely blank. There had been substantial changes to our share structure and staffing levels, but the creative part of the application – the programme ideas – had withstood the IBA's scrutiny. In many cases applications for franchises were written not by the people who would end up running the show, but by dewy-eyed idealists whose far-fetched (i.e. costly) programme proposals were quickly jettisoned as commercial realities crowded in. But the Ayrshire application had been a personal vision of local broadcasting, and with the IBA's insistence I was being given an opportunity to prove that the vision could be made to work. I had promised more talk programmes than the average ILR station and an extensive commitment to outside broadcasting: now I would deliver.

On October 1 1980, I took up my new job as managing director of an unborn radio station on a starting salary of £15,000 – beyond the dreams of avarice after so many years of BBC penury. We could even afford to feed Vesuvius once or twice a week. The board had appointed Bill Fyfe as commercial director, probably hoping that he would keep an eye on me and that we might not hit it off. Initially we used Bill's house as our office – unlike the study of Maybole Castle it was centrally heated day and night – and I did much of the early planning sitting cross-legged on the thick carpet of his living room while Bill continued to supply janitorial services.

Pleasant as this arrangement was, we could hardly run a radio station from Villa Fyfe. When an Ayr builder went bust and his offices and workshops were offered for sale by the receiver, we promptly commissioned an architect's report.

The only problem with 54a Holmston Road, Ayr, was psychological rather than practical. As our next-door neighbour we had the local cemetery with its grand archway which Margaret nicknamed the Pearly Gates. The gallows humour became a little wearisome. Job applicants who referred to the "dead centre of town" and prospective disc jockeys joking about "raves from the grave" were discouraged.

From my vantage point in the boardroom I enjoyed an unimpeded view of the more spectacular funerals. The masonic ceremonies were particularly impressive in their slow majesty. Once a piper's lament permeated the boardroom during a discussion about our overdraft. The directors failed to appreciate the irony.

So we had an address; and soon the builders were knocking the workshops into studios. What we still didn't have was a name. The IBA had, to our chairman's dismay, ruled out Radio Ayrshire for

The Closing Headlines

the odd reason that it wished to avoid confusion with a BBC station of the same name. We protested, reasonably enough, that there was no BBC station of the same name; nor was there likely to be. Then Brompton Road thought of another objection – the ILR station in Leeds had been baptised Radio Aire. We continued to protest, but on this matter, as on so many others, the IBA was immovable.

Radio Ayrshire was dead. Long live...?

Some radio stations were named after local rivers, but Radio Doon had a discouraging ring and was certain to encourage quips about Radio Doom (the one next to the cemetery). We thought of prominent hills no longer than it took someone to surmount Radio Mullwharcher. Radio Ailsa, in honour of the volcanic island off Girvan, sounded better until we were reminded that Ailsa was also the name of a local psychiatric hospital. Sillier and sillier, the suggestions rolled in. Radio Scotland West? Too resonant of a telephone book. Radio Rabbie? Land O'Burns Wireless? Burnside Broadcasting Corporation? Don't call us, we'll call you...

Before Christmas we were joined by our head of news Robin Wyllie, a fast mover with whom I had worked at the BBC.

"We need a name for this station, Robin."

"West Sound," he replied crisply.

The IBA, anxious to avoid confusion, accepted West Sound. So successfully did the authority avoid confusion that soon the ILR network claimed a West Sound in Ayr, a Radio Aire in Leeds and a Radio West in Bristol. An advertising agency boss wrote a letter to a trade paper claiming we were all mad.

Until the end of the year, the two executive directors typed their own letters (or rather I typed Bill's), answered the telephone and acted as doormen. Visitors, however, were so few that they were events in their own right. "Who's that?" I asked one quiet winter morning. Bill went to the window. "Looks like the dustman." But when the figure appeared in our chilly quarters upstairs, it was not the dustman, but a comic from the Gaiety Theatre, Ayr, looking for a job as a disc jockey. (Enterprise was rewarded: he got one.)

In January we became six. Ever the economist, I hired our latest recruits on government training programmes. Our two graduate newcomers searched in vain for a pen or paper or something to occupy them; at length the eager pair were sent out to undertake "audience research" while 16-year-old Lorraine Dante stayed at Holmston Road to make the tea. I think she uttered her first word six months later. In the Spring our outside broadcast unit arrived, early enough to be used for training staff, and the disused warehouse started to resemble a modern studio complex with state-of-the-art technology. We were given our waveband frequency – 290 – and a provisional launch date of October-ish. My wife went to Habitat to buy some cheap but stylish furniture for the reception area. The countdown was on.

And I had filled the clean sheet of paper. The programme schedule did not look significantly different from the theoretical one which we had submitted to the IBA a year before – but with the essential difference that there were names attached. The raw inexperience of most of them alarmed me.

I left Robin Wyllie to lick our broadcasters into shape, and concentrated on marketing. From all I had read and heard, I was convinced that the fate of our little station would depend largely on what happened to us in the first week. There were few exceptions to the rule that if you didn't get it right immediately you would never get it right; and hard experience had shown that an audience which failed to listen at the start was unlikely to be converted later. It was instructive to study case histories of struggling stations whose output was at least as good as more successful rivals, but which had been doomed by ineffective or non-existent pre-launch promotion. I persuaded the board to let me have a generous marketing budget and, instead of spreading it thinly on a mixture of press and poster advertising, went for broke with our own 12-page newspaper which the Post Office undertook to distribute to every household in Ayrshire.

The strategy nearly came unstuck because of IBA intransigence over the on-air date. Jim Donaldson explained that until the authority's engineers confirmed our technical readiness no firm date would be forthcoming. But surely these Code of Practice tests were a formality? Donaldson in his quiet way disabused me of that notion. The IBA's boffins had been known to delay starts, even to order studios out of commission. We must take nothing for granted.

I tried to force the pace. I rang Thompson's deputy, Peter Baldwin, and cheekily named our date: Friday October 16. I explained that we were up against a printer's deadline for our launch newspaper. We were ready; how about the IBA? Baldwin listened sympathetically, but reiterated that he could not pre-empt the code of practice. It was late September 1981, and IBA engineers were crawling over the building. Dare I risk it? Unless we printed now, the Post Office could not guarantee delivery by October 16. Hang it all. We'd print.

Three days later, they began ripping the studios apart for the umpteenth and last time. I waited in the office until they finished – I would have waited all night. Just before midnight they came upstairs with the verdict.

"Well?"

"You're OK. It's the 16th."

What the IBA never knew was that 150,000 newspapers confidently stating the date had already been produced.

16

Why does my Pekinese keep fainting?

Elvis Presley sounded more like Pinky of Perky fame when Radio Forth's hapless disc jockey played the first record at the wrong speed. At Clyde, the studio broke down as soon as the newsreader opened his mouth. Impressed by these tales of launch-day horror, I arranged to start West Sound with a prayer and hope that the great programme controller in the sky was on our side.

On the stroke of 5pm, I made a brief announcement which sounded terribly Bee Bee Cee by the racier standards of ILR. A dog-collared gent blessed one and all. Then two primary school children unveiled a plaque in the main studio and, in tremulous unison, declared the station open. Robin Wyllie read a longish news summary. Someone else read telegrams. Tony Currie, who had presented Clyde's launch programme, was listening to us at home with growing disbelief; would this lot ever stop talking? After 15 minutes Bryce Curdy, our senior presenter, finally cued the first disc (Abba's "Arrival") – in Currie's opinion a British all-comers record for ILR stations.

Outside the studio a jolly party was in progress. Our directors and shareholders were celebrating and it appeared that they had invited half of Ayrshire. I selected a few of the more distinguished names for interviews. Sir Andrew Stewart, a former controller of BBC Scotland, was warm in his praise for the idea of local radio – "just a distant pipedream in my day" – and Bill Morris, the IBA's member for Scotland, promised an expansion of ILR into the Highlands and Borders. George Ffitch, managing director of LBC, expressed surprise that nothing had gone horribly wrong – "so far" we added simultaneously – and dear old Jameson Clark recited a splendid ode which he had written in honour of the occasion.

At 8 o'clock the station's soulful theme tune brought the party

The Closing Headlines

to an end, and like all good parties it ended with one of the guests in tears. Letitia Donnelly, an Ayrshire teacher, wept copiously when she heard her composition played on air. She had entered it as a jingle for a children's programme at a time when, fortuitously for both of us, I had been driven to despair by commercial demo tapes arriving on spec from London sweat shops. "West Sound's the best sound" breathed choirs of sexy-sounding girls. In return for such flattery one enterprising studio boss had the temerity to enclose an invoice. I binned the lot and sent for Letitia. Her pupils at Glencairn Primary School, Stevenston, hummed the melody, Mystical Waters by name.

How many out there were listening, apart from Tony Currie? Certainly not our guests. We received several calls – the staff of Brodick Post Office on the Isle of Arran got through first – but the real test of the station's popularity was still to come. As I left the studio, tripping over the empties, the disturbing thought occurred to me that we would somehow have to keep this show on the road 14 hours a day, seven days a week, 365 days a year, with a small, overworked, and painfully inexperienced staff. Like the Windmill, we would never close. It didn't bear thinking about.

A reporter from the Sunday Standard, God rest its soul, joined me at the red hexagonal desk in the studio reception area for the start of our first full day. "Here to do a sketch for tomorrow's paper," Gordon Petrie explained. The Dolphin Club had just popped its head above water and, so far, was swimming smoothly. Fiona MacDonald, assistant presenter of the children's show, invited young listeners to call and Jean Falconer, my secretary and general factotum, stood by the telephones, more in hope than anticipation.

What happened next was colourfully reported by Gordon Petrie in the Sunday Standard:

Kenneth Roy, director of Britain's newest commercial radio station, shook his thatch of silver-grey hair in disbelief. "Overwhelming," he remarked, as around him a handful of the 30 staff of Ayr-based West Sound frantically struggled to cope with a mounting barrage of telephone calls.

The air waves were proving unexpectedly choppy yesterday morning as, it seemed, most of juvenile Ayrshire attempted to take part in the station's first phone-in programme. The Good Ship West Sound, launched with a three-hour live party on Friday night, was facing up to its first full day of broadcasting and all was not quite plain sailing.

No one had expected the huge response the young public was to make to the children's Dolphin Club. West Sound's switchboard was jammed from the moment it opened. Among the callers was the Post Office to say the town's main telephone exchange was in some difficulty because of the volume of business.

At the receiving end of all the attention was just one West Sound telephonist. She faced a Herculean task of answering calls, jotting down dedications, coaxing youngsters to part with names and addresses, as well as encouraging the suddenly star-struck to go on the air.

In Studio A, children's club host Lou Grant was experiencing all the problems of running Ayrshire's answer to the Multi-Coloured Swap Shop on his first-ever major radio programme. On more than one occasion, all his resources of quick thinking and repartee from 20 years as a stage comedian were called on as he found himself talking to callers who had already rung off.

He rose manfully to the task of trying to encourage an 11-year-old girl to take part in a Yes/No quiz where the youngster was expected to answer questions without using the two fateful words. The child responded by saying nothing at all to Lou's questions and the quiz was dropped till next week.

The morning's star caller turned out to be an eight-year-old girl who wanted to know why her aged Pekinese kept fainting. Strain on the heart and its age, the station's vet suggested tactfully. A diagnosis that could have applied at that moment to some of the West Sound staff. While bedlam raged on behind the scenes, Lou, aged 43, was presenting an unruffled voice to a potential 300,000 listeners from Skelmorlie to Ballantrae and countless thousands in Glasgow and beyond who can pick up the transmission – sandwiched between Radios 1 and 2 on the medium wave.

Somehow he managed to take instructions from the telephonist in his headphones, cue in records, read dedications, carry on a conversation with his guests, and play commercials all at the same time. Listeners were certain to forgive him the one audible slip when he introduced himself after a news break as Lou West of

The Closing Headlines

Grant Sound.

At 11.03am, after two hours on the air, Lou emerged slightly shell-shocked from his studio to a helping of Bold John Barleycorn that would have delighted Tam O'Shanter.

The weekend which began chaotically ended chaotically. Late on Sunday afternoon, I collapsed into a studio chair and fell asleep. A pre-recorded programme was on the air, while the inexhaustible Robin Wyllie – who turned his able hand to everything – had started to piece together the first edition of the chairman's classical music series. It seemed that nothing further could go wrong.

I woke up feeling like death.

"I don't think these will do," Robin said. He was gazing disdainfully at a pile of R.D. Hunter's 78s.

"What's up with them?" I asked drowsily.

"Just listen." He flipped one of the discs – ancient enough to be called a gramophone record – on the turntable. The cacophony of scratches might have been acceptable on a domestic machine, but played through a modern broadcast system, it was intolerable. The din reminded me of Shaw's observation that he would rather have his teeth drilled than listen to a piano recital. It had to be faced: these antiques were too far gone to be any use.

Unhappily for us, the chairman had recorded the links for his programme, At Home with Hunter, and could not be contacted. The programme was billed for 7pm. It was now 5.30.

"Is there anything you can salvage?"

"I suppose enough for 30 minutes." (Half the advertised length.)

There was nothing else for it: John Carmichael, amiable presenter of the preceding programme, Sounds Scottish, would have to cover the hole. He improvised brilliantly, even managing to crack a joke about R.D. Hunter being expected home at any moment. The chairman rang later in an apoplectic fury. It was an acute case of that familiar complaint of our trade, scrambled ego.

After pacifying R.D. Hunter, I sat alone in my darkened office at the far end of the building. Across the wall, only the taller headstones were visible in the gathering gloom. It was 8.30 on a Sunday night in October, and although we had shut for the night the managing director's tranny was still tuned loyally to 290. Our place on the waveband permeated dead air – a strangely peaceful atmospheric. What was it James Gordon had said? "You'll spend all your time putting out fires." West Sound was 48 hours old, and already I had extinguished a few.

Anyone in the team who wanted to broadcast got a chance: with 100 hours a week to fill, we could ill afford to be choosy. Bill Manson covered golf, Robin Wyllie did a jazz show in his spare time – although spare time was foreign to his nature – and Jean Falconer, when she was not typing letters, presented My Kind of Country, the most popular of our early evening music programmes. Kathryn Thompson, a young Canadian who had the infectious habit of beginning sentences with the word "anyways", was among the most industrious people in the building: single-handedly she produced the local commercials and had enough in reserve to front a folk music programme.

We hired a few old pros. Glen Michael, a seasoned TV performer, introduced his first Sunday requests programme by yawning – a risky thing to do on radio – and Jameson Clark compiled a series of interviews with prominent Scots. I shall come to another old pro in the next chapter. But small stations operating on shoestring budgets depend on creating their own personalities. One of the pleasures of the job was seeing untried talent flourish.

Before the start, I had been disenchanted by the daily batch of demo tapes from eager young hopefuls, most stuck in a depressing groove of slick, vacuous DJ-speak without a glimmer of originality. "Don't you realise," said Tony Currie at one point, "that you could get them to work for nothing if you wanted?" Quite so. But the prospect of a poor man's Radio 1 or a poorer man's Radio Clyde was unthinkable. I was committed to finding a distinctive voice for the station, and one way of achieving it in our music programmes was to reject the adolescent sound of pop-driven stations. We hired grown-ups.

As a result, some unlikely people became minor stars. Probably the most knowledgeable musically was Allan Andrews, a process worker at the BP oil refinery in Grangemouth. In his letter, he made it clear that he had no ambition to be a professional disc jockey; he collected vintage popular music and simply wished to share his enthusiasm with like-minded others. Over the years he had amassed thousands of records from the 1950s and 1960s; I cannot remember how many thousands, but it was enough to make me wonder about the creaking floorboards of his bedroom-cum-record store in Stenhousemuir.

Allan was not only a fervid collector, but a walking encyclopaedia of popular music with the gift of instant recall. Yet he had no broadcasting experience, even in the traditional recruiting ground of hospital radio. I put that right by offering him a Sunday lunchtime programme celebrating the music which he had made his life. A superb technician, he mastered without fuss the difficult craft of self-operating a studio, and unobtrusively created order out of the chaos of our record library. He was an asset.

In time I was able to offer him a staff job. Thousands of part-time disc jockeys would have leapt at it; not a few would have sold their grannies down the river Doon. Allan Andrews, with almost courtly good manners, asked for time to think about it. A week later, he told me that it wasn't for him. He continued to present his programmes for West Sound between shifts at the refinery, and I imagine that in his perfectionist zeal he is still pursuing some elusive track by Alma Cogan or Ruby Murray. He must be one of the few people who has ever turned down a break into full-time broadcasting.

Another of our discoveries, Tommy Truesdale, cut an extraordinary figure in his drainpipe trousers and crepe soles. Ayrshire born and bred, he lived in the seaside town of Prestwick, but Memphis, Tennessee, would have been more his style, particularly during the era of his great hero, Elvis Presley. If Tommy Truesdale had been a year, not a man, he would have been called 1956.

He earned a living as a vocalist with a band called The Sundowners. Though a complete professional on stage, as a radio disc jockey Tommy Truesdale was a technical catastrophe waiting to happen. He faced the console with all the confidence of a nervous teenager preparing for his first driving lesson, and there were times during his Sunday afternoon country music show when one feared that poor Tommy might be about to die in five minutes flat. Yet his chronic insecurity before the microphone endeared him still more to his fanatical supporters.

When I received our first audience figures, the results for the Tommy Truesdale show made bizarre reading. They almost amounted to a breach of the new sex discrimination laws: so few young men listened to the programme that the audience in this category was too small to be measured. The number of middle-class listeners for Tommy was also much lower than the station average. Not to put too fine a point on it, his audience consisted more or less exclusively of middle-aged, working-class housewives with an insatiable appetite for The Old Rugged Cross. And there seemed to be an endless supply of such women; he regularly attracted a heavier post than any other West Sound presenter, as he never tired of reminding me.

Once he had controlled his fear of the machinery, he relaxed into a highly idiosyncratic mode of presentation. His folksy delivery included the unaffected use of the archaic form "Mistress" rather than "Mrs" when he was reading listeners' letters. Then, one Sunday, Tommy's wonderful mistresses disappeared. When I complained that the programme had lost part of its charm, he replied sadly that a colleague had drawn his attention to the peculiarity and he was unable to revert to it. He would feel too self-conscious.

The last time I saw him in the studio, at that somnolent hour on a Sunday afternoon when the culturally unreconstructed women of Ayrshire had finished the washing-up and were resting by the hearth listening to sad love songs on the radio, Tommy was bent-backed over the console, his profile a wistful study, a packet of cigarettes and an overflowing ashtray at his side. Remind him of the new no-smoking ban? I had not the heart. He looked so content in his melancholy.

And then there was Lou West of Grant Sound, hero of The Dolphin Club's baptism of fire, Bill Fyfe's dustman at the door when no one called at Holmston Road except mourners. A comedian to trade, he was a Scottish version of Woody Allen with hints of Inspector Clouseau. His mid-morning show, almost anarchic in its incompetence, made me groan. But I had overlooked one vital ingredient: the most vital ingredient for success in broadcasting.

"My," said Bryce Curdy as Lou went through his disorganised paces, "that's one warm wee human being."

With Lou Grant, all conventional judgements had to be suspended. He was not a disc jockey and did not pretend to be a disc jockey. He was vulnerable and made mistakes. He sounded like one of life's losers, and people identified with him. The trick was not to impose the normal professional disciplines on such a performer – that was a lost cause, anyway – but to remove all the obstacles in his path except the banana skin which was his stock-in-trade. After a few months I decided that he must be given the peak-time breakfast show, which in its original format had not been a great success.

Some of the directors thought I had gone mad. Two bought me strong drink and advised me to let sleeping comics lie. The IBA's Scottish management went one better with a cautionary lunch. I held out, and laid a bet that Lou Grant at peak-time would win exceptionally high ratings. That was bravado. I knew perfectly well that I was taking a huge risk which might backfire badly.

Lou, who possessed the good comedian's fertile imagination, had devised a number of novel features for his new programme and, as with all his ideas, they carried an element of danger. He invented a pipe band ("the boys") who gave persistent over-sleepers what he called a "tranny blast". It would not have appealed to my sense of humour at 6.25am, but fortunately it appealed to Ayrshire's. He was inundated with requests for tranny blasts, and some listeners demanded to have a word with members of the band. Using a tape of discordant voices and his own natural gift for improvisation, he had succeeded in creating a private world of fantasy populated by invisible people.

His musical policy, in so far as he had one, was eccentric. He tended to favour sentimental Irish tenors and hymns. Loud pop music ("heid-bangin' stuff" as he called it) was taboo except for purposes of ridicule. He was not really interested in music at all, except as an occasional diversion from the essential business of the morning – talking to the audience, as comics do.

One morning, he announced that he had mislaid a tape. Would everyone mind hanging on while he looked for it? Off he went, humming a gentle tune, to rummage in some distant corner of the studio, leaving his listeners suspended open-mouthed over their corn flakes. Whatever next? But when an audience asks "Whatever next?", it is hooked. Nonchalantly Lou strolled back to the desk and resumed his running commentary as if nothing had happened. It was a brilliant device, intuitive rather than calculated, which used the medium as few other presenters would have dared to use it. Unpredictable and perverse, he was far removed from the stereotyped ILR presenter. With Lou Grant on the loose, the studio was as big as a stage – and it was set for a virtuoso.

Upstairs the sales manager fretted. "That Lou Grant talks too much. Not enough music. Just chat, chat, chat. What people want is Top 40 music and snappy news bulletins. It'll be a disaster in the ratings, I'm warning you now." I ignored the warning.

Big George, the night watchman, known to Lou as "chief security officer" replaced the pipe band. He was introduced as a monosyllabic bearer of coffee with a slightly sinister smoker's laugh, but soon Big George was promoted from cameo role to star status. At 7.30 the programme came to a halt while Lou devoured another of Big George's disgusting breakfasts. "A disaster, I'm warning you."

After a while, Big George went the same way as the band – Lou had a variety artist's sixth sense about the need to refresh the bill – and a regular phone-in caller, Jimmy from Maybole, became chief foil. Something in Jimmy's doleful rural tones and his inability to answer simple quiz questions appealed to Lou's sense of the absurd, and the pair developed a surreal double-act. The secret of its popularity was the dropping of clues, each more bizarre than the last, about Jimmy's identity. We discovered that he owned a parrot, kept a mistress, and wore yellow wellies. Before long Jimmy from Maybole wellies went on sale in local shops, and Jimmy from Maybole jokes were raising big laughs at the Gaiety. He was the stuff of local legend.

Did he exist? I too lived in Maybole, but I had never heard of a Jimmy who fitted the exotic description. I suspected that the character was a plant – a crafty stunt on Lou's part. But then Jimmy asked him whether he could come to the studio. Lou agreed – a mistake, in my view – and to everyone's amazement he appeared at the front door in a flashy new Volvo. I was careful not to discover the truth about Jimmy. For years afterwards I half-expected to see a man walking down Maybole High Street with a parrot, a peroxide blonde and a pair of yellow wellies. I would have turned discreetly away. Jimmy from Maybole and the Pekinese who kept fainting had this much in common: like so much good radio they were better imagined than experienced.

17

Sandy's Indian summer

Fifteen years after I first heard the irascible voice of Sandy Webster, the former editor of the Sunday Mail called to offer his services to my (unborn) radio station. Could this silver-tongued charmer be the same tabloid bully who once sounded so offputting that I stood him up rather than go for a job interview? The paradox intrigued me. This time I would see him.

When we met he was much as I had pictured him – pugnatiously small with craggy lifeworn features and a tweed jacket as old as the Carrick hills. He smoked too many high-tar cigarettes and enjoyed a double whisky at noon. He fitted almost too snugly into the stereotype of the hard-bitten hack.

We lunched at Fouter's Bistro. Sandy loved on sight the atmospheric little restaurant converted from the disused vaults of a bank in a lane near Ayr harbour, where the smell of the sea was exchanged for the tangy aroma of Laurie Black's sauces. But there was one sauce which my guest declared missing. "Where's the sauce of Harold Wilson?" he bellowed as the winsome Fran Black approached.

"The what?"

"Must have some HP sauce. Fetch it, would you, there's a darling."

"This is Mr Webster," I interrupted. "He might be coming to work for us."

"Really?" said Fran. "That's nice."

That day, as most days, Sandy did most of the talking. His speciality was quick-fire interrogation with running commentary.

"What's the best paper in Scotland?"

"No idea. Tell me."

"Sunday Post, of course. Bloody obvious it's the most

professional. Now explain why."

"It panders to our weakness for the couthy."

Sandy snorted. "Never changes, that's why. Got the formula right and kept it that way. Punters love it. Take a tip from the Sunday Post for your wee radio station. Get the furniture in its place and if the punters like the look of it, don't move it around."

As I discovered later, Sandy disliked popular newspapers. The Post won his respect for staying loyal to its principles, the classic family newspaper as inseparable from the Scottish Sabbath as unswept streets and the toll of Calvinist bells. But the papers which had "moved the furniture", his own Sunday Mail included, he held in fastidious contempt. He told me that he had given up newspapers because he could no longer tolerate Page 3 pin-ups and other forms of journalistic vulgarity; he confessed that he would have liked to edit the Glasgow Herald more than anything else in the world.

But that first day we talked mainly of radio, not newspapers. What were my plans? How could he help? Was there anything to be done by an old man with nothing left to prove?

He unfolded the story of his former phone-in for Tom Steele's Radio Forth: how he berated middle-class Edinburgh and how they loved every minute of it. His broadcasting technique was to be as rude and disagreeable as possible; remembering my first contact with him in 1966, I could well imagine. But now he was living in Largs, his wife had died, he was alone and kicking his heels. Why not give Ayrshire listeners an "open forum" in which to vent their opinions and prejudices? Webster would have the last word, of course.

Over the boozy lunch at Fouter's I became infected by his boyish enthusiasm. What would he say to an hour in the late morning? "Make it two," he pleaded. "Want to play some of my favourite music. Love music. Never gave me music at Forth."

Gently I explained that music was not part of our plan. The programme we had in mind for that slot would include a phone-in on topical issues, but it would also report the news of the morning as it happened. We wanted to exploit the resources of Independent Radio News, an agency service for which we were paying handsomely, and to get our own reporters on the road, feeding back material live from a Land Rover. Sandy expressed lukewarm approval of the idea.

"Sure, the news of the morning. Great idea. But just one thing, Ken."

"Yes?"

Imploringly: "You'll allow me one or two records, won't you?"

By the end of the lunch we had agreed that he should present three two-hour programmes a week (with music) and that I should sit in for him on the other days. Over brandy we dealt with the only business so far unspoken.

"What's the pay?"

"Oh, I thought you were doing this for love."

"For love and money. What's the pay?"

"Name your price."

"Mustn't interfere with the pension rights. Settle for 50 a week on one condition."

"What's that?"

"I can take my guests to lunch at Fouter's."

Sandy became a frequent visitor to the embryonic radio station, cheering me up by playing the clown. On one of many days when nothing was going right in our preparations for the launch, he whisked me off for an informal promotional tour of Ayr High Street, buttonholing any passers-by who were prepared to listen.

"I'm Sandy Webster – one of the West Sound team."

"Good for you" was the droll reply.

"Take notice," he said to the next. "This man here is Kenneth Roy. You've heard of Kenneth Roy, haven't you?"

"Don't believe I have."

"He's the boss. And *I'm* Sandy Webster. Remember the name."

Occasionally the comic mask would drop for no particular reason. Facing each other across the boardroom table he stamped out a cigarette and uttered a prophecy.

"You'll end up lonely. It's inevitable. It'll happen. It happened to me. At the Mail I used to close the office door behind me in the morning. and I could have sat there all day without seeing a single soul. Of course, I got *them* to come to *me*. But that isn't the point. It's the loneliness of the job. You'll see."

★

Soon after he volunteered to join us, Sandy announced that he proposed to move to Ayr. Largs was "a bit far from the office" and he had taken a shine to the leafy suburb of Doonfoot, which he pronounced Dinfit. Rather than answer house ads in the paper he had marched up to a door at random and asked the householder (a woman) if she would sell him her flat. She wouldn't, but gave him the name of someone in Dinfit who would. He left with a deal.

Ever the master of surprise, he disclosed that he would not be alone in his flat. He was about to marry Ina, widow of a close colleague on the Sunday Mail. "Isn't that wonderful?"

This was the start of Sandy's Indian summer of 1981. He had a new job, a new house, a new town, new colleagues, a new wife. He was a happy man. But he was also losing his sight. "How does it feel to have hired the world's first blind DJ?" he joked. "Well, you don't have to see to answer phone calls on the radio," I joked back. But it was no joke. He had more or less given up trying to read small print. Newspapers were increasingly difficult. The news as it happened? I supposed that could be delegated to one of the reporters. As for scripts, he never used them. But he would require the names of the callers to be written down in extra large print on narrow strips of paper. Fiona MacDonald, his assistant for the first few weeks, did this for him and an enormous magnifying glass also helped.

As our on-air date approached, Sandy took to calling at Holmston Road on his way home from the shops. He badgered me mercilessly. "When do I start earning ma pay?" "When do the dummy runs start?" "Have you got my studio finished yet?" "Why isn't there more in the papers?" "Where's the bloody drink?"

At a pre-launch production meeting of all the presenters, he appalled the innocents with sardonic asides about the inadequacies of the programme schedule, the ineptness of the management and the green appearance of all concerned. It was Webster at his histrionic peak, middle of Act II stuff, but only I knew that. As the meeting rumbled on into the afternoon, he pretended to be asleep, grunting at any particularly fatuous comments. Finally the old gent sat bolt upright, lit a ciggie, and rasped: "What about the racing tips?"

The company fell silent.

"Forget your community involvement and your jobspots and all that nonsense. What about ra punters?"

When Robin Wyllie finally admitted that no provision had been made for racing tips, Sandy slumped back in his chair. "Nae racin' tips," he sighed. "Och, aye."

At home, the charming Ina by his side, his alter-ego emerged: the civilised man of the world, gregarious and hospitable, in place of the maddening provocateur and whisky-sodden journalist who'd seen it all. After dinner at Dinfit one evening, Sandy, resplendent in black velvet jacket and purple bow tie, played the piano most tenderly. Later he took me aside.

"You won't want me for very long, Ken, now will you?"

"On the contrary, I've constructed the schedule around you."

"That's a mistake. I'm an old man."

Before the evening was over he returned to the topic but in a rollicking style. "Roy's a slave driver," he roared. "He wants me to go on for ever. Can't you just see the headline? 'World's oldest DJ dies at mike'." We all laughed, and Sandy did a party turn – a mock interview with Margaret on a cassette recorder. But the message was not lost. He had given me a warning.

On the morning of his dummy run he strode dramatically to the small office I had reserved for him, and demanded what Bill Fyfe used to call janitorial services. Newspapers! Scissors! Coffee! Girls! Producers! Soon the atmosphere in the room was blue with smoke as well as electric with tension. Keeping well away, I assumed that nerves had got the better of him and that by 11 o'clock the old trouper would have settled. But when I went downstairs to see how his off-air debut was going, the show had still not begun.

Sandy, installed in the studio with his guest, Paddy Harris of the Scottish air show, had the demeanour of a deranged bear not long escaped from the zoo. He had removed his jacket, revealing the world's loudest-coloured braces, and his bow tie, though still nominally attached to his neck, had been carelessly undone along with the first two buttons of his shirt. He was wearing a set of studio earphones and, completing the vivid picture, a green eye-shade. The morning papers, cut to ribbons, lay scattered across the studio round-table and with his magnifying glass he was studying what remained of the Glasgow Herald. From his mouth drooped a magnificent cigar.

"Ready Sandy?" inquired Robin Wyllie, cold as a fridge.
"Ready! Ready! *Been* ready for half an hour!"
"Cue coming."
The theme music, sonorous and funereal, suited the mood. Sandy launched into a hopelessly extended introduction: a rambling monologue. "N–o–w", he said finally. "I think I have a guest." It was true: the guest, though older, was still alive. But instead of interviewing Paddy Harris, Sandy delivered another monologue on the future of Prestwick Airport and refused to let Harris have a word in edgeways. With his next victim, Bill Manson, he was even more boorish and incoherent. Exasperated, I spoke firmly to him on talkback.
"Would you mind getting to the point?"
There was no response; with half an hour still to run Robin and I agreed to abort the dire rehearsal. Sandy rose from his seat looking as kindly as a hanging judge and walked head-high from the wreckage of the studio. Back in the office, I was told that he wished to see me. His jacket and bow-tie had been restored, and the cigar had been replaced by his usual brand of cigarettes. He looked more fretful than angry, although it became clear that he was very, very angry. He began by tendering his resignation. I refused it.
"You and I are not going to get on," he said flatly. "You don't belong in the commercial radio game. You're a BBC man." (This was a familiar line; he was fond of calling me Howard M. Lockhart after a polite BBC announcer – the ultimate Webster insult.)
"You're right. But that's my problem."
"Why didn't you like the show this morning? There was nothing wrong with it. Damned good programme."
"Not for me."
"It's the best I can do. It's the *only* thing I can do. It's *me*. Whether *you* like me or not."
"You went completely over the top. Not only that, you kept interrupting your guests. You wouldn't let them speak."
"Don't talk rot."
I sent Jean Falconer out for a bottle of Johnnie Walker and over a meandering afternoon we made up. I had a hunch that, whatever demon it was that Sandy had just exorcised from his system, it

would not recur. And I was proved right. His first show – his real debut – was the talk of the town. Big George, our night watchman, returned from the pub with the unanimous verdict of the drinking classes: "Wha's that Sandy Webster? Cheeky bugger!"

In taxis, shops and streets he was an instant talking point. He infuriated, offended, occasionally even flattered. But he shook Ayrshire out of its complacency. He set people talking – not only to Sandy but among themselves. He was the man who would talk about anything. Want to talk about World War III? Go ahead! Dying to make a point about the uncollected rubbish at the bottom of the street? Then be quick about it! The juxtapositions of topic and mood were brutal; in any other than the skilled hands of this practitioner – and Sandy has had many crass imitators – they would have been embarrassing. Fools or bores were cut off in their prime. "Heard enough of you! On to my next call!" He was loved and loathed in more or less equal proportions. There was something about him that went straight to the heart of the community we were serving.

Before his first programme of the New Year, he came to see me. "This will be my last. Blood pressure's shot through the roof, and the doctor's ordered rest. Sorry, Ken, but the phone-in's a killer. I'm smoking 20 fags in two hours down there."

I decided not to replace the irreplaceable. Over an anguished weekend we devised a new formula which altered the emphasis from topical affairs to listeners' practical problems. Celia Stevenson and Fiona MacDonald worked hard to establish their programme as a credible successor, but the switchboard operator struggled to cope with callers demanding: "Whaur's oor Sandy?"

After an absence of four months, Webster's phone-in returned to West Sound once a week. The volume of calls was not as great: no more did he emerge triumphantly from the gladiatorial ring thundering: "58 calls, and not one disc!" His insistence on the right to include records had been a cover in case there were disappointingly few calls; now, at last, the lover of music had time to play some. And the programme had lost much of its energy and pace; Sandy suddenly sounded like the old man he was. A spell had been broken.

But there were agreeable compensations. In that tired, mellow delivery was distilled a lifetime's experience. If a radio event no longer, he had become a connoisseur's delight.

He was seldom seen. He did his programme, acknowledged his friends, and left. My own contact with him diminished, but one summer morning he wandered into my office before the programme. I was in the middle of a long call to an IBA bureaucrat. In more robust days he would have given me two minutes before leaping from his perch with some ribald remark. This time he stayed until I had finished.

"How are things?" he asked.

Unusually for him, he made flattering noises about the radio station, shrewdly identifying its strengths but saying little about its many weaknesses. Slowly he turned the conversation round to himself. "I'm so very lucky," he said. "Ina's marvellous, and I'm happy with my wee job. Couldn't ask for more."

I heard later that after the programme he sat motionless in the reception area for a long time. Finally someone offered to call him a cab. He returned to Dinfit and rang friends and acquaintances he had not seen for years. Next day, a few hours before he died, two members of the staff met him up town and exchanged a few pleasantries. "See you next Wednesday at the station," one shouted cheerfully.

"God willing," Sandy replied.

18

"You'll end up lonely"

Cunninghame District Council challenged us to stage the biggest Burns Supper in the world. An enumerator of Burns Supper attendances estimated that a crowd of 700 would be required to beat the record held by a comradely gang in Moscow. But local caterers quailed before the prospect of keeping 700 haggises (haggi?) hot. A compromise was reached: we would stage half the biggest Burns Supper in the world and hope to stage the other half next year.

I called Jameson Clark. "Leave everything to me," he said, in that voice as comforting as Scotch broth. Within hours he had booked the main performers: Moira Anderson to sing; Lord Willie Ross for the Immortal Memory; the Rev. James Currie to "do" the Lassies; and Jean Taylor Smith, a fine old stage actress, as respondent to Currie. In the end Jean decided that she was not up to the ordeal and recited a Burns love poem instead. I drafted a terrified Fiona MacDonald, aged 23, from the West Sound staff to take her place.

A reconnaissance of Irvine Co-operative Hall an hour before the start suggested that, although we were not yet staging the world's biggest Burns Supper, we might be able to claim the world's longest top table. Stretching half-way to Kilwinning, it offered severely limited room to those sitting behind it. As things were, Willie Ross's legs would be entangled in the criss-cross of the trestle and Jimmy Currie might end up on Jean Taylor Smith's lap. I did a spot of strategic re-positioning, taking care to remove a place card naming Dr Macdonald, Moira Anderson's husband, "Mr Anderson".

A long queue had formed at the entrance. Why the jam? Soon the explanation was only too visible: one of our top table guests,

The Closing Headlines

too infirm to walk upstairs to the hall, was being fork-lifted by two elderly volunteers. I knew there was a Dr Macdonald in the house. Was there also a Co-operative undertaker?

In the anteroom where our guests were gathering, I knocked back a stiff whisky and was told that my face had turned puce. A piper began his wailing. We arranged ourselves into a prefects' queue for the off. Inside the hall, John Carmichael and his band were playing as if their lives depended on it. Silently I cursed the spirit of the bard. Just then, Robin Wyllie appeared looking like the ghost of Suppers past. "What's up?" I squeaked.

He gave me it straight: "We have overbooked. There are 40 members of the public standing outside with tickets but no seats. The hall has been checked. Every seat is taken."

"OK, OK, put in more seats."

"Impossible. No room. Can't be done."

"Have you talked to the people outside?"

"I have, and they're in an ugly mood. There's a shop steward type threatening big trouble."

The revellers fortunate enough to have seats had downed Cunninghame District Council's free miniatures long ago, and the hubbub of their conversation reverberated in my aching brain. Still the piper wailed. What to do? Eric Dale, a member of the station's advisory council, approached me in a spirit of amiable concern. "For God's sake, Eric, I'm doing my best. Have patience, won't you?" Eric looked shocked. "Now, now, Kenneth," he said. "Now, now, now."

Poor John Carmichael, last spotted bailing me out of the At Home with Hunter debacle, had been asked to warm up the audience with a short medley. "Got a bit of a problem," I bawled, straining to be heard above the din of yet another reel. "Me too," John bawled back. "We're running out of material." "Too bad," I said. "Just go back to the beginning and start again." And the band played on.

Meanwhile I had a brainwave. If 40 must be counted all the way in, 40 must be counted all the way out. A check of West Sound personnel and friends identified just enough candidates for eviction. They were shunted into an overflow lounge and pacified with drink. During the speeches, connecting doors were opened and the refugees enjoyed a squint-eyed view of the toasts.

The Closing Headlines

When the top tablers finally entered the hall, a roar went up and we were slow-handclapped, though in a friendly way. Our chairman rose to make his introductions and, too late, I remembered that there had been several last-minute withdrawals. R.D. Hunter, sticking to his brief, welcomed a member of parliament who was unexpectedly absent. "He's no' here," a wit hooted from the back of the hall, "unless he's under the table."

Gloomily I hid behind the programme. With a speech to deliver, I could not risk getting even moderately tight. At least we were now ready for the first item on the running order, the Selkirk Grace; in four hours, with any luck, I would be in bed. The reciter of the Selkirk Grace leaned over my shoulder. "Do you think we should go ahead with this?" he demanded. "Probably not," I said sardonically. "Good, because I can tell you, you're making a big mistake. Robert Burns never wrote the Selkirk Grace." With murder in my heart I told him that I couldn't care bloody less who wrote it. (But who did?)

Despite these moments of high farce, it turned into a marvellous evening and, in its modest way, a historic one. It was the last time that three outstanding Burnsians – Jameson Clark, Willie Ross and Jimmy Currie – shared a public platform. Soon, all were dead. But if I listen hard I can hear echoes of their swan song: Jameson delivering Tam O'Shanter as rousingly as it was ever delivered, Willie in the full glory of his oratory as a Burns scholar, Jimmy preaching the gospel through laughter and a sparkling joy. Whatever happened to the body on the stairs, I didn't dare to ask.

Local radio, if it is doing its job effectively, should be the hub of its particular universe. With the Burns Supper, a schools quiz, debates, and even a live Hogmanay programme from a Prestwick hotel, we took the show on the road as we had promised in our application to the IBA, and brought the station to its listeners.

And we were lucky: within a few months of going on air there were several unexpected opportunities to prove ourselves as a valuable alternative to the BBC and Radio Clyde. When word reached us that the Secretary of State for Scotland, George Younger, was to make a Commons announcement on the outcome of the UK Atomic Energy Authority's controversial proposal to dump nuclear waste in the Galloway hills, we cleared the decks for an open-ended programme combining Westminster reaction with studio discussion and including Celia Stevenson's report from our O.B. unit on how it felt to be alone in these desolate hills as dusk fell. Produced by Robin Wyllie, the programme demonstrated a flair often lacking in formulaic local radio, and brought together many of the leaders of our scattered community. When Younger announced that he had turned down the UKAEA, Gibson Macdonald of the local Tories hugged the SNP's Ron Wylie in common cause (a sight seldom seen, I think). For two hours, the new radio station was where it was at.

Then the Falklands crisis broke, and ILR managing directors were summoned to London for an urgent briefing at the IBA. This was instructive as well as depressing. Most of the Perrier-sipping suits around the conference table in Brompton Road were less worried about how to cover the war than about the inconvenience of having to cover it at all. General Galtieri and Margaret Thatcher had chosen to confront each other on the high seas at just the moment when local radio stations were squaring up to a war of the airwaves, the annual JICRAR survey of audience ratings. Better leave the Falklands to the BBC than risk losing listeners seemed to be the consensus, and it was not actively discouraged by the IBA's radio officers.

It struck me forcibly that day how few broadcasters ran ILR stations. There were salesmen aplenty, some accountants, others of no fixed background or, for that matter, obvious qualifications for the job. They might just as well have been producing baked beans, and judging by their crude perceptions of our trade they probably thought they were. James Gordon was a brilliant exception, but there were not many others. I listened in disbelief as these shoddy characters, with the apparent connivance of the IBA, attempted to wriggle out of their public responsibility to report Britain at war.

From a pragmatic point of view, I doubted whether listeners would be readily budged from their favourite station, Falklands or no Falklands, but it was conceivable that an ILR station which provided intelligent coverage of the war might actually gain listeners. There was the further consideration that it was being fought at a distance of 6,000 miles and, thanks to the obduracy of the Ministry of Defence, facts were scarce. Was Ayr, then, at so much more of a disadvantage than London? We were able to draw on IRN, which had men in Buenos Aires and Washington as well as with the task force; we had access to the same Westminster debates as the BBC; and we even had a local angle – one of the local MPs, George Foulkes, had risked national opprobrium by speaking out against British military involvement.

For all these reasons – but mainly, as always, for the hell of it – I was determined that we should do our own thing. At the height of the crisis, we truncated Lou Grant's breakfast show, leaving a trail of unrequited tranny blasts, and substituted a daily programme bringing local listeners up to date with overnight developments. We milked the IRN tapes, invited MPs into the studio, analysed press coverage of the war, and had our own resident expert, Jim Pirrie, a community education worker in Kilmarnock, who had spent 12 years in the Falklands as an itinerant teacher.

The sales manager was horrified that we were turning ourselves into an all-news station as JICRAR conducted the audience research on which our future revenue critically depended. I pointed out that whenever we ran a Falklands 'phone-in there was an unusually heavy response. He was unconvinced. "Bring back the recipes," he implored. We didn't. And after it was over, many people made a point of telling me that, although they hadn't listened much to West Sound before, they were impressed by our coverage of the crisis and would stick with us. Jim Pirrie sent a first-day cover of Falklands stamps as a token of appreciation. The IBA rang to commend our enterprise.

An unknown American golfer, Bobby Clampett, was leading the Open Golf Championship at Troon on the day of the JICRAR results. We were running a two-hour programme about the tournament every afternoon in defiance of an R. & A. ruling that we must not broadcast more than two minutes an hour. Any more, the press officer warned, and we would risk an interdict. Charming. I told him to stuff our accreditation, reluctantly granted to us in the first place; we would pay at the gate, report the championship freely, and challenge any interdict which might come. None did. Bill Manson and Celia Stevenson did a splendid job in the lowest traditions of piratical journalism.

A golfer who reached the turn at Troon in 35 strokes was doing reasonably well, but a JICRAR score of 35 would not be much good to us. "Reach" – an expression of the percentage of the available audience listening at any point in a given week – was what impressed advertisers, and reach could vary from 20 to the upper 60s. In our case there was a complication: because Radio Clyde penetrated so deeply into our territory, the industry assumed that West Sound's reach would be relatively low. A national sales agency in London said that we should regard a figure in the mid-40s as a triumph, guaranteeing us a more generous share of the advertising cake. Unproven, we were receiving only crumbs; and our financial position was perilous.

All morning I hovered nervously by the phone. Peter Baldwin, the IBA's deputy director, had likened it to waiting for one's exam results. And at 1pm they came.

"Richard Tillett here. Thought you might like to know the outcome of your JICRAR research."

"Hmmm..."

"Of course you understand we only have the top-line results at the moment. But so far as the main figure's concerned, West Sound has achieved a reach of 56%. A very good result, one of the best in the network. Congratulations."

It was nine months to the day since we had gone on air, and the little station that few had given a ghost of a chance was among the most popular in the country. Veronica McDowall, our IBA officer, treated me to a celebratory lunch at Fouter's and said candidly that West Sound was now the authority's blue-eyed boy. At the end she asked whether I had ambitions to move on.

"Maybe once I had. Not now. I'm sticking around to build on what we've achieved. For ever, probably."

Three months later I was fired.

We had started in the depths of a recession. In Bill Miller's opinion this was an excellent time to launch a business; he argued that if you could survive a recession, you could survive anything. A year later, however, the economy was no livelier. National revenue, generated from London ad agencies, was disastrously below our optimistic projections. Radio had been so poorly promoted by the industry that many of the larger agencies regarded it as a fringe medium, almost as a joke. And what money there was in the system certainly wasn't heading towards Ayrshire, a marginal area covered by an existing and much larger ILR contractor. "Buy Clyde and you buy the West of Scotland" was the received wisdom. Why spend on Ayrshire's David when Glasgow's Goliath could do the job for you? The question haunted us.

Our impressive ratings helped a bit, though not as much as we had hoped or been led to believe. Meanwhile, the once-buoyant local economy was hard hit by liquidations; Ayrshire had acquired the unenviable distinction of the highest unemployment rate in industrial Scotland. When times were bad, businesses spent their way out of trouble. But margins were now so squeezed that, for many, advertising was no longer an option. In desperation I fired the sales manager and hired another. It made little difference. The overdraft continued to soar and the share capital was exhausted. If only we had heeded John Thompson's warning about the perils of under-financing. If only...

I confided the seriousness of the position to Robin Wyllie. "The operation was successful," he said softly, "but the patient died." It just about summed up our plight.

Yet we were not quite without hope. The economy must improve sooner or later and when it did we would be all right. Surely, too, our ratings triumph would eventually be reflected in higher sales. And if I spoke nicely to John Thompson, the IBA might cut the rent in order to ease our cash flow. After all, the authority had staked a great deal on West Sound as a proving ground for similar experiments in overlapping a small rural station with a larger city one; it would not want to see us go down. We should hang on in there.

All this might have consoled me. But the malaise went deeper than the purely financial. From the moment before we won the franchise when Miller held his pen over the staff structure and I made my tactical retreat as putative managing director, I sensed that I was not their man. Only the IBA's insistence that I should be MD, in effect as a condition of being granted the franchise, had restored me to the job. My fellow directors prided themselves on being a "strong, commercial board", hard-headed men of the world who expected a quick return on their investment, and within that framework a broadcasting chief executive sat uneasily. "Kenneth is a superb broadcaster and a good administrator, but has no commercial brain," one director wrote.

There was truth in this criticism. I was so stung by it that I spent much of the next 10 years acquiring business skills. How silly. In return I might have criticised the board for not supporting me strongly enough when Bill Fyfe, my deputy, who did have a commercial brain, resigned several months before we went on air to take up a major public appointment as chairman of the Ayrshire and Arran Health Board. He should have been replaced, but he never was. "You'll end up lonely." I did. With Bill gone, Sandy dead, and relations with the board far from cordial, kindred spirits were few.

On our first anniversary Julieanne Stevens and Timothy Bradbury, the children who had launched the station, were invited back for a special edition of The Dolphin Club. They cut a cake. We received many cards, telegrams and flowers; a local wine merchant sent champagne. But I could not help noting the silence from our board of directors. Perhaps they had forgotten. Perhaps not. I submitted a trimmed budget for the next financial year, and some rang to say they approved.

A week or so later a deputation arrived – the men in the grey suits of political legend. Two of the hatchet-men were local accountants. Only the third member of the party surprised me – a breezy operator called McNaught, principal of a teachers' training college. I had thought the chairman, Hunter, or his deputy, Miller, might have had the decency to fire me in person. Instead our resident brainbox had been given the dirty work. How low of them.

"We have some information for you," McNaught began.

Before he went on, I said that he could spare his breath and that I had been alerted by accident to their treacherous meeting the previous evening at Hunter's house; that I had been tempted to exercise my director's right to join them. "My dear chap," he replied airily, "you would have been made most welcome. It wouldn't have made the slightest difference to anything that was said."

"Naturally" the board's first concern in "restructuring the management" had been "your kind self": he deferred at this point to one of the accountants, who outlined the pay-off terms.

I addressed my only question to McNaught.

"Tell me just one thing."

"What's that?"

"What did I do wrong?"

He replied after a pause: "You didn't do anything wrong."

I left on the spot and, 11 years later, have not been back; nor have I listened to the station since that traumatic day. The hurt went deep.

For their own reasons, all my closest colleagues followed within a short time: Robin Wyllie back to the BBC; Fiona MacDonald to Carrick Publishing as my deputy; Celia Stevenson to Scottish Television; Jean Falconer to local journalism, until that bonny fighter succumbed to cancer; Jim Brian, the chief engineer, to set up his own business.

There were no immediate departures from the board. Later the company diversified into private nursing homes, a growth industry during the governments of Margaret Thatcher, and Bill Manson resigned as a matter of principle.

19

Sort of anonymous

The obituaries read nicely. The boys brought me the Sunday Standard in bed on the first day of the rest of my life, and there I was at the top of the front page next to the splash. Could this really be me? The ghastliness of it all had not penetrated yet, though we had switched off Vesuvius as a mark of respect and in sombre acknowledgement that we could no longer afford the beast.

Being unemployed was not a unique experience. When I was 17 and it was 76, the Falkirk Mail died on me; at 18 I was fired by a horrid newspaper for going on holiday without permission; and the immediate aftermath of leaving Reporting Scotland might have qualified as unemployment. But then, I had something in mind – a plan. Now, I was – what was that humiliating word the papers used to describe people on the dole queue? Ah, yes. I was "idle".

This was the late autumn of 1982. Less than a decade later, hundreds of thousands of other managers would have found themselves as I was, on the scrapheap, clueless what to do next, worried sick about money. But in the late autumn of 1982, 37-year-old down-and-out executives did not make many headlines. I felt intensely isolated, as well as bitter, disorientated, and betrayed; later, when managerial sackings became the norm, I learned from the papers that these were the classic symptoms of people "in my position".

Former associates were kind. John Thompson spoke at length from the IBA and hinted that, if I had called him the moment I heard, something might have been salvaged. He sounded eager to keep me within ILR and offered to recommend me for managing director posts in England if I was interested. James Gordon, my old adversary, said over the phone that he would like me to work in an unspecified capacity for Radio Clyde. I was grateful for their practical concern and said that I would contact them when I was feeling up to it. I didn't.

A curious item appeared in the Glasgow Herald. "Ken will be looked after," an anonymous spokesman for BBC Scotland was alleged to have said. Shades of the godfathers. Sure enough, my old patron George Sinclair showed up. I wept tears of self-pity over lunch while he entreated me to return to my former beat. I said that I would contact him when I was feeling up to it. I didn't.

I had a summons from my bank manager. Very understanding he was, too. In my own interests it would be best if I cleared the little matter of the outstanding overdraft while I still had my silver handshake; bang went £2,500. The rest – about the same – we frugally earmarked to keep us over a chilly winter in Maybole Castle while we looked for somewhere more in keeping with our reduced circumstances. Eventually we scraped up just enough to buy a quarter of a grand house on a hill overlooking the town. Out of work I had no hope of a mortgage, but Robert Gardiner, West Sound's solicitor, who was dismayed by the turn of events, gave me a loan on generous terms.

On a still and wonderfully clear Guy Fawkes night, we let off fireworks on the castle lawn. The Marquess of Ailsa's factor had decently agreed to release us without penalty from our long lease; we would not be here much longer. I had been away from the job less than a fortnight, but already the West Sound years were misting over into weird unreality. What had happened to all those spring mornings and lazy summer afternoons, high days and holidays, the natural boundaries and punctuation marks of life, while I pursued the not-so-wonderful obsession? Gone as if in a dream. And the obsession itself, I saw now with dull clarity, was as meaningless, as instantly forgotten, as the dampest of Guy Fawkes night squibs.

For a long time I did nothing. Three gruelling years had brought me close to "burn-out", that phenomenon of late 20th-century society in which over-achievers drain themselves physically and emotionally while serving implacable gods. How I longed to drop down some hole in the ground. But wounded dogs hide more easily than has-been personalities; anonymity for us is an endangered state constantly threatened by invasion. "Didn't you use to be Kenneth Roy?" someone asked.

In January 1983 I moved into a small office in Miller Road, Ayr, sharing the top floor with Ken McKeown, an accountant who was starting out in private practice. It was a sedate district. A few doors along, the Ayrshire coal miners had their rooms. During the miners' strike of 1984 the lights burned long into the night. Then the strike ended in abject defeat, the pits closed, and one night the lights weren't burning there any more. Opposite my front window, a sad old hotel where the last of the miners played darts after their shift was turned into a night club called Bonkers. Bonkers, indeed.

I resurrected the publishing idea. After a few false starts which tried the patience of creditors, the business took off in a small way. The recession had ended: even people with no commercial brain could make money out of the Thatcher boom years, but in my case. not enough initially to draw more than a nominal salary. When the BBC beckoned me back, like a lamb I went.

The department of miracles no longer bustled with ideas. Paul Streather was dead, Donald Macdonald had left, and Ian Mackenzie spent more time than ever in remote Sutherland hotels contemplating the future of the universe or drawing up 10-year plans. A great one for 10-year plans was the head of religious broadcasting; if only he had been a member of the Politburo, Soviet communism might still be flourishing. In his absence I found myself working with younger, more conventional people on a routine Sunday night series called Voyager. Despite its title, the programme rarely took off.

For a long season I was ubiquitous, presenting not only Voyager but the Friday evening political programme, Agenda, with the former nationalist MP, George Reid. I tried to make friends – it helps if one is on nodding terms with one's co-presenter – but Reid was the coolest customer imaginable and we exchanged few words. He might once have addressed me as "mate", which I took to be progress of a sort. Later he left to join the Red Cross in Geneva, and I presented the programme solo. I failed to miss him.

Apart from the distant Reid, the current affairs department was a lively, congenial place. I had worked for it only once, years before, when David Martin gave me a precious half-hour to explore a topic of my own choice for the series Current Account (known to insiders, inevitably, as Current Bun). God help me, I chose the Church of Scotland. When he saw the rushes, the experienced Martin acutely went to the heart of what was wrong with the film. "This isn't a story," he said, "it's a subject." He had just rendered the Book of Revelations in seven words. But it was too late to do much about it.

After the thing went out, one of Current Account's regular reporters, Kenneth Cargill, was generous in his praise. "I wouldn't have believed you could have made such an interesting film on such an unpromising theme," he said. (Lie.)

Now, 10 years on, Cargill frae Arbroath was George Sinclair's deputy in news while Matthew Spicer – gifted, kind, caring Matt – continued to preside over the current affairs department which he had been running ever since most people could remember. With him were some of the nicest, cleverest people in the BBC: Tom Ross, Alf Young, Carol Craig, Stewart McIntosh, Val Atkinson. I looked forward to Fridays for the company, even if the programme veered unsatisfactorily from orthodox current affairs to specialist political coverage in the same 30 minutes. All of us would have preferred to concentrate on the politics, but there was an increasing suspicion that the post-Hetherington regime viewed current affairs people as subversive lefties.

In this belief the new regime was partly right, partly wrong. We did lean to the left (few BBC programme departments did not), although one of our number drooled over pictures of a beautiful Tory MP, Anna McCurley, who subsequently lost her seat to some dull Labourite. Nevertheless, it would have been improper to suggest that we could not be trusted with politics. We were professional journalists, not party hacks, an important distinction which our masters might have neglected, borne down as they were by La Thatcher's attacks on the BBC's independence and on the whole ethos of public service broadcasting.

I did not know, nor did I wish to know, the new controller who was sometimes irreverently referred to as a pig farmer from Aberdeenshire. I assumed this was a joke until I checked his entry in Who's Who and discovered that, among other things, he was indeed an agriculturalist of some distinction.

Matthew Spicer, who might usefully have stayed at home to defend his patch, went off to make a series for BBC2 about the politics of other small European nations. He discovered on his return that the department was about to be abolished. Matt was summarily removed from office, just as the presidents of some smaller European nations are removed. However, unlike them, he was not shot at dawn. He was merely taken to the newsroom and sat in a corner.

With Matthew Spicer gone and the department swallowed whole by news, the programme was clearly doomed and morale sank. Good people drifted off, and we were told that Agenda would soon be replaced by a Sunday breakfast slot with an all-star cast. I was not quite top of the proposed bill, but pretty close to it. Then someone – Mackenzie, perhaps – came to me with worrying news. At a meeting of some internal programme review board, my name had cropped up. How did people think I was doing? A florid Ulsterman whose name escapes me – to do with sport, I seem to remember – had criticised my "grey" persona and there was a feeling that since the West Sound experience I had "gone off slightly". Ominously the controller had nodded agreement.

"But it's nothing to worry about," said my informant cheerfully. "Your usual supporters backed you to the hilt."

The grey man was listed in Radio Times as a co-presenter of the Sunday breakfast nonsense. There was an accompanying feature which mentioned me in passing. But on the eve of a press conference for the new Scottish political programme – reduced now to a cornflakes and pyjamas ghetto – Kenneth Cargill rang. There had been a change of plan. I was not to be a co-presenter after all. I would, however, contribute items from time to time. And, he added without enthusiasm, I was free to attend the press conference as planned. Because I liked and admired Cargill and because I had been here before, I made no fuss. I simply said that I would not be attending the press conference or contributing items from time to time, and left it at that. Who said that history repeats itself, the second time as farce? This was farce.

My absence from the canapés-and-plonk reception was noted by inquiring journalists and for the second time in a year the newspapers went on the scent of a Roy sacking. Who said that to lose one job in the same 12-month period is unfortunate, but to lose two sounds like carelessness? This was careless.

"What will you do now?" asked Andrew Young of the Glasgow Herald.

"I'm going to Cumbria for the weekend," I replied. "Then I

have a business to run."

"What business is that?" said Andy.

We fled south and, at Carlisle, read all about me. On Monday, when I returned to the office, I doubled my monthly drawings from Carrick Publishing and advertised for a secretary. I could afford neither an increase in drawings nor a secretary, but forced back on my own resources, all crutches removed at last, I had precious little alternative. And at this point I risk sounding like one of those dreadful self-improvement manuals about how to succeed in business. By applying the lessons I had learned the hard way at West Sound, I succeeded in business. I had been taught by experts.

We published some good books, some bad ones, started a journal which continues to flourish, and made decent profits. Nine years later the secretary I couldn't afford, Linda Holland, is still with me. Another recession came and we survived it. So far. Always we must add "so far". But I have not been anyone's puppet. Nor will I be. This is the only promise worth making.

A sort of anonymity descended. No one asked me to broadcast. I was happy. "Aye, son," said a man in Maybole, "they did a bad thing when they got rid o' you." Could it have been Jimmy? Whoever it was, he could not have been more wrong. They did me a favour.

20

Small country

In July 1991, Bill McCue, the opera singer from Shotts, did a brave thing. As part of a BBC Scotland series, The Scottish Tradition, he attempted to interview Jimmy Shand, the octogenarian band leader and accordionist. Where he went wrong was in imagining that he could break down the verbal defences of Auchtermuchty's most famous son. Old Shand fully justified his reputation for elevating the humble monosyllable to the status of abstract art.

Imprisoned in a set which might have been inspired by Anthony Hopkins' cage in Silence of the Lambs, Bill McCue tried every trick in the book: flattery, gentle teasing, encouraging laughter. In extremis he even dared to suggest that he and his guest had a lot in common. It was difficult to tell if Jimmy agreed: Jimmy wasn't saying. But then, Jimmy wasn't saying much about anything.

About his musicianship, the lovely man had least of all to say. "It was a new technique you were developing," Bill McCue prodded him. "Ah wouldna' say it was new," Jimmy mumbled. So the conversation turned to the exciting places he had visited during his long career. "All over," Jimmy replied. Indeed: all over in more ways than one. But with another 20 minutes to fill somehow, Bill pressed on. What about hobbies? Hadn't he been a keen motorcyclist? He had.

"Aye," said Bill, "there's no' many hedges you havenae been over in Auchermuchty."

"Ah wouldna' say that," Jimmy replied.

"What were your other hobbies?"

"No' many."

This was the point at which a lesser interviewer might have been dragged from the cell, screaming for a merciful injection of gas pellets. But not the intrepid McCue.

"Where did you keep your boat?" he persisted.

"Wormit."

"Where did you sail?"

"In the Tay."

"You never ventured into the deep blue sea?"

"Nut."

Well, that seemed to be Jimmy's hobbies all wrapped up: in a nutshell, as it were. Only Bill McCue had ventured into the deep blue sea, and he was drowning fast.

The other half of BBC Scotland's pawky hour that night was concerned with the rather less exciting hobby of gardening. The original Beechgrove Garden team had been pensioned off, and the corporation's weeds in Aberdeen were being tended by Bill Torrance and Carole Baxter, assisted by Jameson Clark's one-time sparring partner, Sid Robertson. "The spring is past now," said Sid, with the air of a man who knows all about the passing of the seasons.

"The spring is past now," Carole answered briskly, "and we're on to summer." Sid nodded knowingly.

Aye, and the tatties were doing well too.

"The tatties," said Bill Torrance, surveying the BBC's patch, "shouldn't they be ready?"

This time Sid shook his head. "Too early," he assured Bill.

"So when do you know they're ready?" Bill asked.

"When they're big enough," Sid said, "they're ready."

Jimmy Shand could not have put it more succinctly, and this magical hour of television had more or less written my television column for me. These were the good weeks, when it was simply a matter of taking it down in rusty shorthand and transcribing it verbatim. But there were not many good weeks in my years as Scotland on Sunday's man before the mast. Usually it was desperate work for a hermit with square eyes and a remote control. One week there was so little worth noticing on British television ("the best in the world" as we were constantly reminded) that I resorted to reviewing the weather forecast.

What is a TV critic for? There must be more to it than an ability to mint wonderful, witty phrases as Clive James did for the Observer or, later, Mark Lawson for the Independent; the best critic is someone like Philip Purser who not only writes knowledgeably about TV but actually enjoys watching it. I was too sardonic after years of working in the industry to approach the job with the sympathy of a Purser; nor was I blessed with the phrase-making gift of a James.

Unlike critics of the performing arts, the TV critic constantly finds himself (or herself, the Guardian's Nancy Banks Smith being the doyenne of the trade) reviewing work which is over and done with before the notice is printed. I doubt whether this form of criticism is of much value, unless the programme is of exceptional interest or has aroused public controversy. Even in these special cases, the reader who missed the programme may feel frustrated by a review which gives him no more than an brief taste.

The impotence of the TV critic and perhaps also the eclectic nature of the remit – wildlife, a game show and Peter Snow one week, a play, a drama doc and Esther Rantzen the next – encourages glibness. Most TV critics are in it to raise cheap laughs, little Clive Jameses but without his occasional insights. In short, TV criticism with a few outstanding exceptions (among them Julie Davidson in Scotland) is not a very respectable branch of journalism – higher in reputation than the travel page and the motoring column but not much.

However, a television critic for a Scottish newspaper is in a more privileged position. He can use his column to hold a mirror to contemporary Scottish society as it is reflected – or, more often, not reflected – on the screen. With the precious freedom granted by an editor, Andrew Jaspan, who never interfered, I discriminated heavily in favour of Scottish-made programmes, especially those with something to say about the way we live now in this small, insecure country on the periphery of Europe.

I discovered from years in a darkened study that Scotland is a very small country. There were times when I felt rather like the character in one of Paul Theroux's misanthropic novels who tried to convince people at a party that the world consists of only a few hundred people; except that Scotland seemed to consist of even fewer. One dispiriting evening I could have sworn that the only person left out there was a West of Scotland poet and playwright, Liz Lochhead.

Between 10.40pm on Thursday August 15 and 12.40am on

Friday August 16 1991, Miss Lochhead appeared in three successive television programmes on the same channel. She had just published a new book of poems; one of her plays was being produced on the Edinburgh Festival Fringe; and, as a young woman of sensitivity and intelligence, she could expect to be in demand. But three in a row on the same night did seem a trifle excessive. When I worked for Reporting Scotland, I formed in my imagination an exclusive club with the acronym SIP (Scottish Instant Pundits); if SIP was still in existence I would have made Liz Lochhead chairman for 1991, with Pat Kane, rock musician, her vice.

For the life presidency of SIP, one required to look no further than William McIlvanney, the novelist who withdrew at a sensibly early stage from the Ayr local radio franchise. He was seldom far away in my four years of box-watching and was a favourite subject of women interviewers in the posher papers.

On News at Ten, a man with a head wound was seen being admitted to a Glasgow hospital. "What happened?" asked the surgeon. "The usual," the man replied laconically. "Attacked by a knife." I brooded over this extraordinary remark for some minutes. If a butcher's knife in the head was the "usual" price to pay for an evening stroll in the former citadel of European culture, it might be prudent to resurrect Pat Roller, the Daily Record's roving crime reporter, and Lord Carmont, the notorious High Court judge who dished out "condign punishment" to violent young Glaswegians.

Thirty minutes later, after the comic interlude of Evening Call, I was still pondering what this man had said. Then along came Jenny Brown, a bright little literary button, with McIlvanney in tow. Undeterred by the latest health warnings, Jenny and Willie were indulging in what ITN had assured us was a very dangerous practice. They were daring to walk the streets of Glasgow.

Admittedly they were not out for long. Willie was taking Jenny to room 102 of the Grosvenor Hotel where he was writing another of his novels which "celebrate the working class" and pontificating to admirers from Scottish Telly about the "humane irreverence" of Glasgow. A nicer place to do this than room 102 would have been hard to visualise. It was anonymous but extremely comfortable. They brought him food. And if he cared to visit the cocktail bar between chapters, or as a break from the latest comely interviewer, he was sure to meet some friendly face from the BBC. As to his chances of being bloodied by a butcher's knife in room 102 before he finished the novel, I would have had to rate them slightly below the city average.

I had agreed with McIlvanney at the Ayr meeting about the need to avoid crap in local radio. One could adapt this statement to cover colour supplements, airport paperbacks, Spanish hotels, junk food, polystyrene cups, downmarket newspapers and other disagreeable features of modern life. But I hadn't agreed with much that he had said since, and I wasn't agreeing with him now.

He claimed to Jenny Brown that "Glasgow tells us what contemporary Scotland is all about". This is a preposterous assumption. Glasgow tells us nothing about the depopulated glens of Sutherland, Edinburgh's emotional emptiness, the self-absorbed lives of Border villages, spiritual certainties in the Hebrides. And his sentimental pigeon-holing made the working class sound like some endangered species fit for inspection by the natural history unit. Did the working class even want to have its humane irreverence celebrated by William McIlvanney? Would it not rather buy its council house, stay in room 102 of the Grosvenor Hotel, and enjoy a drink with the lovely Jenny Brown? I posed these questions in the paper. Few responded.

Scottish television's (with a small t) acceptance of silly statements and sillier deeds by the high heid yins of our narrow society, its generally acquiescent tone, its matey familiarity with those in power or positions of cultural influence, its intellectual sloth and lack of curiosity, its sheer timidity, irked me so intensely that the 1,000 words a week for Scotland on Sunday's back page with its sideways layout of my sideways opinions were often splenetic. One reader, Anne MacDuff, wrote to the editor to ask whether I approved of anything on television. This was unfair, but not grotesquely so.

The nadir was reached with the ill-advised live transmission of the BAFTA Scotland awards on Scottish TV in November 1991. Early in the proceedings McIlvanney appeared on the podium of a spectacularly vulgar set to collect the "Best Single Play" award and announced in a voice husky with emotion that the winning script had "given a voice to people in our society who have been sadly under-valued – teenagers" – a cringe-making testimonial surpassed only by Emma Thompson's dedication of her 1993 Oscar to the whole of womankind.

Next, a police serial produced by Scottish Television won "Best Drama Series". That a panel of informed people seriously considered Taggart, all grisly ketchup in beetroot factories, the "best" of a whole year's output said everything that needed to be said about our shaky sense of identity. A cynical piece of commercial gore, it was tricked up for no other motive than to satisfy an ITV network controller's stereotyped vision of Glasgow – the same muddled stereotype which so excited visiting reporters from ITN and novelists in room 102 of the Grosvenor Hotel. Here was the urban flipside of the equally improbable rural couthiness represented by Take the High Road, a soap opera set among the pinned hats and ghillied absurdity of some mythical lochside village.

Of course it is not all down to the network's distorted vision of Scotland. There is a quality in the Scots themselves which masochistically enjoys the gross caricature of our personality. It expresses nationhood with a snigger. It is responsible for Taggart, the busybodying Mrs Mac in Take the High Road, and the slavering Rab C. Nesbitt, he of the bandaged heid, string vest and crude jokes. Such stock figures from popular mythology are part of a long tradition; they are the modern equivalents of the funny kilted Scotchmen who graced or disgraced the English music halls in the first half of this century. They have nothing to do with representing Scotland as it really is, since to do that would be to render us unrecognisable in the south. They are not about art at all. They are about marketing.

For the Nesbitt series, BBC Scotland's comedy unit won "Best Light Entertainment Programme" and "Best Actor" and was shortlisted for "Best Writer"; in addition, the head of the unit – an Englishman – received a gong for an "outstanding contribution" to TV and film in Scotland. It was hard not to laugh. It was harder not to weep.

The same week, Arthur Miller gave one of his rare television interviews. In his preoccupation with individual responsibility – the gulf between what we think we are and what we do – Miller might almost be counted one of us; for an American Jew, he is a fair imitation of a Calvinist Scot. "People say, where is the great modern play? The question is: where is the pretty good play? Out of that yeast comes the important play, the great play," he said.

To echo Miller: where was the pretty good play in Scotland? In the theatre? Having given up going, I couldn't say. I could only say where it was not. It was not on the short-list for the BAFTA Scotland awards, and it was not on television. In more than 180 weeks of professional viewing (1989-93) I saw not a single outstanding play or drama series which originated from Scotland with the possible exception of the embryonic Gaelic serial Machair (Scottish TV). I would defy anyone of discrimination to name another.

Our finest writers work for the page, not the screen or (I suspect) the stage. Why? One possible explanation is that BBC Scotland's drama department has been headed for too long on a part-time basis by Bill Bryden, a man of versatile talents who is also associate director of the Royal National Theatre. Once the jewel in Queen Margaret Drive's crown, the department has produced nothing of consequence since Tutti Frutti (1987). The department is ossifying and cries out for more vigorous leadership. (As this book went to press, Bryden resigned.)

A week after the BAFTA fiasco, the Scottish Writer of the Year award, for which Norman MacCaig had been tipped, went to a London-based novelist, William Boyd, who was not born in Scotland, does not live in Scotland, rarely writes about Scotland, is not published in Scotland, and does not contribute in any meaningful way to the life of Scotland. Appropriately enough, the literary king of our midden was awarded the accolade in his absence. Why do we do it ourselves? What terrible insecurities motivate us?

Here is part of an answer: it relates to our fear of being thought provincial. Deep in the Scottish psyche, our poor little dispossessed psyche, London always knows best. So we fling literary prizes at semi-detached Scots who have been to Hampstead for a hallmark while stay-at-home artists shiver or starve. And in the same mean spirit we cravenly acknowledge the exported sub-culture of quaint Scotchmen who earn a gold star from London, while ignoring programmes which address, and are themselves part of, a community with valid traditions and a continuing life of its own.

Time and again in Scottish literature, London turns up as the place where the talented Scot goes or wishes to go. It is more than a destination, it is a symbol. It is liberty of a sort. The Glasgow Jewish playwright, Cecil P. Taylor, still badly missed, said to me that he always breathed more easily once he had crossed the Border (into England). I understood that. I also understood why the Scottish journalists I met in London would never return. The pain of having to belong would be too much; it must be nice to live where nobody kent your faither. And besides, London is still the place where the arts, literature, broadcasting and journalism are taken seriously. The journey remains necessary. It shouldn't be.

The last poem in Norman MacCaig's collected poetry – the book that didn't win – talks about the journey in reverse. Home – Edinburgh – is creeping closer. MacCaig lights a cigarette and sits smiling in a corner of the railway carriage:

> Scotland, I rush towards you
> into my future that,
> every minute,
> grows smaller and smaller

It need not be so. If only we had the confidence to turn inward to our own enclosed society, as so much of the best literature and drama has done, we would discover that a whole world is revealed to us. But try telling that to the people who control television in Scotland. The network rules, and it is not OK.

"The basic thing is the word," said Miller. "The word is a higher thing than the picture." We should remember that. Even people in television should remember that. But they don't. They are still out there in the cold waters of the Clyde dragging another body from the river while some catatonic inspector of polis stands by. Close up. now. Let's see it decompose...

In the first week of 1992 I was writing about Hogmanay television when I developed a sharp stabbing pain. Not in the neck, which would have been a reasonable human response to Hogmanay

The Closing Headlines

television, but more ominously in the ribs. In agony I coined one last phrase which even Clive James might have been proud of: I described Cathy MacDonald, the presenter of the BBC show, as "the ubiquitous Gaelette". Though it was not intended unkindly, it offended some readers.

Struggling for breath I was taken – "rushed" as the tabloids would say – to hospital and put on an oxygen mask. I was fairly close to death for a few days and, during one bad night fever, half-thought that I might be gone by the morning.

After I was out of danger they gave me a room of my own. Donald Macdonald came with a socialist tract, and I had a breezy visit from the chairman of the local Health Board, old janitorial services himself. I discovered the delights of a personal stereo, but only once tried listening to the radio. It was early on a Sunday morning and a cold-sounding journalist from the Sunday Times was attempting to defend the closure of the Ravenscraig steel works. This was the stuff of which relapses were made. Angrily I switched him off.

A young nurse, a very caring man, said that he would fetch me a television set. I said not to bother. Oh, he said, it was no bother. He would bring the set. And, to please him, I pretended to watch a programme. It was some very randy Melvyn Bragg drama about a middle-aged man who falls in love with a girl, and it was without merit. Yet I noticed in the papers that it was the big new thing; I supposed that if I had been well and writing for Scotland on Sunday I would have had to find at least 500 words to say about it. I decided that I would not write about television again. But, after a while, I did.

21

Epilogue

If you could make it through the first hour – the dancing girls and the tartan comics, the manic audience, the desperate conviviality of the occasion – without developing a sharp pain in the ribs, around 1 o'clock on New Year's morning you would see BBC Scotland's head of religious broadcasting with his sad, crumpled face. And, above some domestic din, you might even hear a few stray words of his message to the whisky-soaked nation. It was always a beautifully crafted script, profound in theme and lyrical in exposition, and yet I doubt whether more than a few hundred people ever listened to Ian Mackenzie's epilogue with complete concentration. Epilogues, like the closing credits of a film or the closing headlines of a news bulletin, are what happen when the audience is getting up to leave, or too drunk to notice, or impatient to be in bed and asleep.

But since the epilogue is a broadcasting tradition at least as old and honourable as those Scottish jigs on a Saturday evening which never fail to evoke nostalgic echoes of my working-class childhood in Bonnybridge, I will not spare you an epilogue. It is written at the end of the summer of 1993.

Twelve years after it went on air, West Sound had its licence renewed – not by the IBA which was abolished as part of Mrs Thatcher's crusade to de-regulate broadcasting, but by a Radio Authority with a "light touch". When the franchise was re-advertised I flirted with the illusion that a few of us would submit a rogue application, if only to give the incumbent a fright. It might not have been such a bad idea: in the end there was no opposition despite grumbles in the local press that the radio station, like Punch, was not as good as it used to be and a report in the Glasgow Herald that it was losing £15,000 a month.

The Closing Headlines

At the BBC, the men who were responsible for Hetherington's downfall are dead and not much missed. Hetherington himself remarried Sheila Cameron, the widow of an Army officer, and spends most of his time at High Corrie, Arran, in a cottage at the foot of Goat Fell, which he climbs regularly. He is 73 and looks a lot younger.

In July, while I was writing this book, Mark Tully, a foreign correspondent with a gravedigger's voice, claimed that the BBC was over-run by fear and bureaucracy. Supporting this argument in Scotland on Sunday, I went on to quote chapter and verse, but pointed out that the cases I was citing related to the period 1972-83 before the present director-general joined the BBC. John Birt, from all accounts, is indeed something of a tyrant but it is important to bear in mind that he is part of a long line of BBC tyrants dating back to Reith himself and including along the way such discredited figures as Charles Curran. The view that the present unsympathetic regime somehow represents a deplorable fall from a sunny upland of liberal enlightenment is the purest fantasy. Fear and bureaucracy are bred in the BBC bone. Ask any grizzled BBC dog who's had his day.

As for this dog, it continued to bark on Radio Scotland until (and a bit after) the farming controller left for Hong Kong in order to be nearer his family. (Could this be true? Evidently.) John McCormick was appointed in his place, and about him I know next to nothing. Greater publicity attended the arrival of James Boyle. According to a profile in Scotland on Sunday, there were now two notable James Boyles in our midst. One was a reformed murderer and the other was the new head of Radio Scotland; the hard man of the two being the head of Radio Scotland. This was a good joke. I laughed.

At the same time I did not envy James Boyle his job. Radio Scotland had been a mess since the start. John Pickles, its first head, was fired after a notorious incident in which, after several too many, he ordered a continuity man to announce that the Queen was dead. He had already messed up the launch pretty comprehensively, but at least Pickles was enough of a broadcaster to recruit a personality and build the station round him. His choice was Jimmy Mack, an engaging if (to some ears) infuriatingly bouncy character who gained a large and devoted following. Only

The Closing Headlines

a management with a death wish would have contemplated letting Jimmy Mack go. But one should never under-estimate BBC Scotland's kamikaze tendencies: Mack now works for Clyde.

The problem was easier to define than to cure: Radio Scotland lacked an identity. Partly this was a result of the BBC's penny-pinching reluctance to promote it. Commercial outfits like my own West Sound had gone on air with a flourish, using public relations skills to involve potential listeners and convince them that the new station should be part of their daily lives. But when had anyone worn a Radio Scotland tee-shirt or been offered a Radio Scotland car sticker? It was a strangely invisible radio station.

While Radio Clyde had "scooped Glasgow patter out of the street and got it on the air", the BBC's alternative sounded tamer, less self-confident, uncertain in tone. A bitter early argument over the occasional use of music in talk-based programmes obscured a larger failure to capture urban Scotland in a broadcasting voice with which the audience could identify. Fourteen years on, this failure had not been effectively addressed: three quarters of the adult population never listened to the so-called "national network".

In a Scotland on Sunday column on November 22 1992, I made these points and went on to outline two priorities for James Boyle. First, he should be given a proper promotions budget and the help of an advertising agency with ideas. Second, he should go talent-spotting for a personality of broad national appeal, someone who would hit the headlines and anger as many listeners as he (or she) delighted, a go-for-broke appointment which would define what the station was about and advertise the fact of its existence. The target seemed plain enough: it was to give Radio Scotland a wider appeal, particularly in urban Scotland. Yet, I noted, James Boyle appeared to be taking a different route. In his first public move, he had decided to emasculate local output from those communities – mainly in rural areas – where Radio Scotland did have a reasonably strong identity. "It sounds like a classic BBC attempt to achieve the worst of both worlds," I wrote, "for it will offend and alienate rural Scotland while leaving the urban problem untouched."

Geoffrey Cameron, a producer I had known and trusted for many years, had booked me to take part in a discussion programme the following weekend. The day after the article appeared, Geoffrey rang and briskly declared that I should consider myself un-invited. He had seen the article. It was extremely unfair to Boyle. I was not giving the man a chance. Perhaps one day I would be welcome back, but not for the moment. I did understand, didn't I?

Here was a paradox. For the programme in question was a live critical assessment of the Sunday press, chaired by Jack Regan with two "leading Scottish journalists" who were requested – indeed expected – to make trenchant observations about newspapers. The implication of Geoffrey's decision was that, while I had every right to criticise the press on BBC Scotland, I was denied the same right to criticise BBC Scotland in the press.

I told Andrew Jaspan, the editor of Scotland on Sunday, of this extraordinary turn of events. He spoke to Boyle who spoke, I guess, to Geoffrey Cameron. And the upshot of it all was an assurance that I had not been banned from Radio Scotland. However, the invitation to appear in the programme was not re-issued; indeed the BBC went on to ask the political editor of Scotland on Sunday, John Forsyth, to take my place. I kicked up a fuss and Forsyth, an innocent party in the affair, was prevailed upon to withdraw.

Since that day I have not been asked to participate in any Radio Scotland programme, apart from a New Year's Day chat show with Edi Stark, which had been half-arranged before the producer knew of the row. Should I, then, go on accepting the official BBC version? Or perhaps I should start believing the Sunday Mail's alternative version with its comic headline inside a funereal border: BEEB BAD BOY BANNED. If I have in effect been blackballed, it is for sentiments milder and more constructive than those voiced by Mark Tully, who continues to enjoy the freedom to broadcast and quite rightly: the BBC should be big enough to accommodate dissenters. But then I have to remind myself that, here in Scotland, such silliness is to be expected. For are we not all rushing towards that future which grows smaller and smaller?

Anyway, I am done broadcasting.

★

The Closing Headlines

In the late spring of 1992, when my lung was recovered and the poor health of the Scottish Tories had also revived unexpectedly, I started my final stint as a television reviewer. I wrote about 20 years of Mastermind, "a symbol of the age when we finally satisfied our thirst for knowing everything and understanding zilch", and about Magnus Magnusson now being a venerable chap of 62; and I remembered the night years and years before when he and I and our respective wives and a few drunken others had tumbled out of Alastair Hetherington's party, having failed to answer the exciting question of what we would do on the morning of Scotland's independence.

The Closing Headlines

Index

Abba, 135
Aberdeen, 22, 169
Addiewell, 25
Agenda, 164
Ailsa, Marquess of, 163
Aitken, Douglas, 104, 106
Allen, Woocy, 141
Alloa, 76
Ally's Army, 107
Ancram, Michael, 32
Anderson, Moira, 153
Anderson, Ross, 24, 100, 103
Andrews, Allan, 139-40
Annan Committee, 56
Arbroath, 165
Ardrossan and Saltcoats Players, 68
Ardvasar Hotel, 49
Argyll, Duke of, 48
Arran, 82
Assembly Hall, Edinburgh, 74, 76, 78-9
At Home with Hunter, 138, 154
Atkinson, Val, 165
Auchtermuchty, 168
Ayr, 111, 117, 119, 127, 148, 172
Ayr Harbour, 145
Ayr Town Hall, 120
Ayrshire and Arran Health Board, 160, 176
Ayrshire Post, 114-116, 127

Bafta Scotland awards, 172-4
Bain, Donald, 28, 35
Bain, Margaret, 35

Baird, Mamie, 54
Baker, Janet, 71
Bakewell, Joan, 71
Baldwin, Peter, 133-4, 158
Ballantine, James, 111-2, 115-6
Ballantrae, 137
Barbour, Very Rev. Robin, 76
Barclay, Campbell, 24
Barlinnie Prison, 63
Barrhead, 50
Barrie, J.M., 68
Baur, Chris, 53
Baxter, Carole, 169
Baxter, David, 102
Baxter, Raymond, 27-8
BBC Club, Glasgow, 52, 66
BBC Scotland: Glasgow newsroom, 19, 36, 45, 102; Studio B, Glasgow, 20; production gallery, Glasgow, 21; Edinburgh newsroom, 36, 45; parochialism of news output, 43-5; arrival of Alastair Hetherington, 46-7; specialist appointments, 52-3; preparing for devolution, 54-7; Glasgow canteen, 66-70; Edinburgh canteen, 71-3; religious broadcasting, 82-4; Studio A, Glasgow, 85-6; dismissal of Hetherington, 107; current affairs department, 164-6
Beau Brummell pub, 73
Beechgrove Garden, 169
Before the Oil Ran Out, 27

182

The Closing Headlines

Benbecula, 104
Benn, Tony, 27, 31
Bernard, George, 13
Berwick and East Lothian
 constituency, 32
Big George (night watchman), 143, 151
Biggest Aspidistra in the World, 68
Biggin Hill, 38-9, 41-2
Birt, John, 178
Black, Laurie and Fran, 145
Black, Peter, 68
Blackhill, 26
Blunt, Sir Anthony, 55
Bob (BBC shop steward), 50
Bob (Glasgow Herald driver), 11, 63
Bonkers (night club), 164
Bonnybridge (aka "Dirty
 Bonnybrig"), 13, 14, 177
Boswell, James, 48
Bough, Frank, 41
Boy from Harris, 15
Boyd, William, 174
Boyle, Andrew, 51-2, 54-6
Boyle, James, 178-80
Bradbury, Timothy, 160
Bragg, Melvyn, 176
Breakish, 49-50, 102
Breich, 27
Brian, Jim, 161
Broadford Hotel, 49
Brodick Post Office, 136
Brodie, Very Rev. Peter, 76
Brown, Craig, 110
Brown, Lord George, 94
Brown, Jenny, 171-2
Brown (R.J.), 18
Brown, Son & Ferguson, 40
Brownsbank, 96
Broxburn, 27
Bryden, Bill, 174
Bryson, Ken, 44
Buchanan-Smith, Alick, 92
Buerk, Michael, 52
Burns, Robert, 69, 122, 153, 155

Byres Road, Glasgow, 66

Cairney, John, 69
Caledonian Hotel, Edinburgh, 35
Callaghan, James, 54
Cameron, Geoffrey, 179-80
Campbell, Gordon, 29
Campbell, Mrs (Margaret), 23
Cape Wrath, 49
Capital Hotel, London, 125
Cargill, Kenneth, 165-6
Carlisle, 167
Carmichael, John, 138, 154
Carmont, Lord, 171
Carrick Publishing, 167
Carstairs state hospital, 104
Cathcart, constituency of, 34
CBI Scottish Council, 113
Chapman, Ian, 121
Charles Dickens (horse), 37
Cheyne and Morrice, the Misses, 102
Children in Need, 107
Children of the Mist, 48
Christie, Bob, 33
Christie, Paddy, 54
Church of Scotland, 47, 74-5, 77, 79-80, 83-4, 88, 164
Civil Aviation Authority, 41-2
Clampett, Bobby, 157
Clark, Bob, 69
Clark, Jameson, 67-9, 135, 139, 153, 155, 169
Clarke, Peter, 53
Clayson, Christopher, 92
Clouseau, Inspector, 141
Clyde Football Club, 110
Cochrane, Hugh, 18, 23-4
Cogan, Alma, 140
An Comunn Gaidhealach, 33
Conn, Stewart, 72
Cook, Fidelma, 54
Coupar, Malcolm ("Mack"), 21, 47-50, 78-9, 102
Craig, Carol, 165
Crawford, Douglas, 35

183

Crossfire, 88-9, 98
Cullen, Alice, 34
Cumbria, 166
Cumnock, 110
Cunninghame District Cll, 153-4
Curdy, Bryce, 135, 142
Curran, Charles, 47, 51-2, 56, 70, 178
Current Account, 164-5
Currie, Rev. James, 82, 89, 153, 155
Currie, Tony, 135-6, 139

Daily Mail, 19, 46
Daily Record, 41, 112, 123, 171
Daily Worker, 30
Dale, Eric, 14, 154
Dante, Lorraine, 133
Danube Street, Edinburgh, 76
Davidson, Julie, 170
Davidson, Kemp, 77
Dimbleby, Richard, 91, 101
Disraeli, Benjamin, 17
Dolphin Club, 136-7, 141, 160
Donaldson, Jim, 121, 127, 133
Donnelly, Letitia, 136
Donnelly, Peter, 99-100
Doonfoot (aka 'Dinfit"), 148-9, 152
Drawbell, James, 92-3
Duncanson, John, 43
Dundee, 35, 56, 112
Dunlop, 82
Dunning (educational reformer), 92

Edinburgh, 22, 24-5, 33, 36, 41, 43, 45, 77
Edinburgh Airport, 35
Edinburgh Festival, 44, 71, 76, 171
Eighth Day, 84-5
English, David, 46
Evans, Harold, 26-7
Evening Call, 171
Ewing, Winifred, 16-17, 35

Faces of Uist, 104, 106
Falconer, Jean, 136, 139, 150, 161
Falconer, Ronnie, 82-3

Falkirk, 13, 93
Falkirk Mail, 12, 162
Falkirk water trip, 58
Falklands war, 156-7
Ffitch, George, 135
Fisher's Hotel, Pitlochry, 62
Fitzgerald, Scott, 93
Five Red Herrings, 126
Ford, Alastair, 18, 90
Forsyth, John, 180
Forsyth, Michael, 30
Forsyth, Roddy, 63
Foulds, Iain, 114
Foulkes, George, 157
Fouter's Bistro, Ayr, 145-7, 158
Fraser, George MacDonald, 16-17, 35
From the Grass Roots, 48
Fyfe, Bill, 117, 128-9, 131-2, 141, 149, 160, 176

Gaiety Theatre, Ayr, 132
Gallagher, Patrick, 118-20, 122, 125
Galloway, small hotel in, 126
Galtieri, General, 156
Garden, Neville, 63
Gardiner, Robert, 116, 163
General Assembly of the Church of Scotland, 30, 44, 74, 75-81
Gibbon, Lewis Grassic, 69-70
Glasgow Airport, 38, 58, 128
Glasgow Bar Association, 16-17
Glasgow Cathedral, 121
Glasgow Central Station, 12, 25
Glasgow Herald, 11-12, 14, 16, 24, 26, 34, 59, 90, 99, 123, 129, 146, 149, 163, 166
Glasgow High Court, 16, 63
Glasgow police stations, 11-12
Glasgow School of Art, 103
Glasgow School of Drama, 86
Glasgow University, 88
Glass, Jack, 76
Glencairn Primary School, 136
Gleneagles Hotel, 23, 67
Good Morning Scotland, 63, 103

Gorbals, constituency of, 34
Gordon, James, 111, 115-6, 120-1, 123, 128-9, 130, 139, 156, 162
Gourock, 23
Graham, Billy, 88
Graham, Rod, 70
Grampian Television, 43
Grangemouth oil refinery, 27-8, 139
Grant, Lou, 137, 141-3, 157
Gray, John, 75
Gray, Very Rev. John R., 76
Great Western Road, Glasgow, 34, 100
Greene, Graham, 15
Greenock Telegraph, 18, 90
Grieve, Vakda, 97
Grimond, Jo (aka "The Great Grimond"), 32-3, 70, 75
Grosvenor Hotel, Glasgow, 171-3
Guardian, 18, 46, 170
Guinness, Alec, 126
Gullane, sands of, 91
Guthrie, Tyrone, 35

Hall, Stuart, 37, 41
Hamilton, Bill, 43
Hamilton by-election, 17
Hannah Research Institute, 114
Hardie, T.L. (Tom), 27
Harris, Paddy, 114, 149-50
Harvie, George, 72
Headlines: the media in Scotland, 123
Healey, Denis, 95
Heath, Edward, 29-31, 33
Heffer, Eric, 92
Heilbron, Vivien, 69
Hemingway, Ernest, 26
Henderson (SNP MP), 35
Herd, Jim, 103
Herron, Very Rev. Andrew, 75
Hetherington, Alastair, 46-9, 51-6, 70, 84, 87, 101, 107, 165, 178, 181
Hetherington, Sheila, 178
High Corrie, Arran, 178

Highland Clearances, 47
Holland, Linda, 167
Holmston Road, Ayr, 131, 133, 143
Home, Sir Alec Douglas, 29-30
House, Jack, 102
Humbie potato-pickers, 26
Hunter, R.D., 110, 114, 122, 124, 126-7, 138, 155, 160
Hunter, William, 99
Hutchison, David, 123

Ibrox Park, Glasgow, 89
Icelandic cod wars, 30
Independent, 169
Independent Broadcasting Authority, 109, 113-34, 142, 152, 156, 158, 177
Independent Radio News, 146, 157
Independent on Sunday, 99
Inside BBC Scotland 1975-80, 47, 51
An Inspector Calls, 64
Inveraray Castle, 48
Iona, 96
Iona Community, 96, 107
Iran, draw with, 107
Irvine, 111, 113, 125
Irvine Burns Club, 111, 121
Irvine Co-operative Hall, 153
Irvine Development Corporation, 111
Irvine Royal Academy, 114
ITN, 173
It's a Knockout, 37

Jack, Ian, 26-7, 99
Jacklin, Tony, 72
James, Clive, 169-70, 176
Jaspan, Andrew, 170, 180
JICRAR, 157-8
Jimmy from Maybole, 143-4, 167
Jenkins, Roy, 95

Kane, Liam, 112
Kane, Pat, 171
Kelvinbridge underground, 100, 102

185

Kemp, Jimmy, 18
Kernohan, Bob, 63
Kilmarnock, 110-2, 121
Kilwinning, 153
Kinnock, Neil, 94
Kirknewton, 27
Kirknewton Gala Day, 38
Kirkwall Airport, 32-3
Knox, John, 74
Knox-Johnston, Robin, 110
Kynoch, Douglas, 20, 24, 43

Labour Party in Scotland, 53
Laidlaw, Renton, 22, 24-5, 72
Laing, Bob, 95
Lamont, Stewart, 88
Larbert milk train, 12-13, 17
Largs, 146
Lawson, Mark, 169
LBC, 118, 135
Liddell, Helen, 53
Lindsay, Maurice, 18
Listener, 48
Lochhead, Liz, 170-1
Lochmaddy Hotel, 104-5
Lockhart, Howard M., 150
Lyle, Sandy, 62 64
Lynch, Bet, 86

McAdam, Carolyn, 88, 104
MacCaig, Norman, 174
MacCormick, Donald, 33
MacCormick, John, 40
McCormick, John, 178
McCue, Bill, 168-9
McCurley, Anna, 165
MacDiarmid, Hugh (C.M. Grieve), 96-8
MacDonald, Cathy, 176
Macdonald, Donald N., 84-5, 88-90, 98, 103-7, 164, 176
Macdonald, Dr, 153
Macdonald, Finlay J., 12-15
Macdonald, Gibson, 156
MacDonald, Fiona, 136, 148, 151, 153, 161

MacDonald, Keith, 109-111, 113, 115-6, 123
McDonald, Sheena, 72
McDowall, Veronica, 121, 158
MacDuff, Anne, 172
McGahey, Michael, 30-1
McGivern, Cecil, 68
McIlvanney, William, 110, 171-2
McIntosh, Stewart, 165
McKay, Johnston, 76
Mackenzie, Allan, 112
Mackenzie, Elizabeth, 107
Mackenzie, Ian, 82-6, 107, 117, 164, 166, 177
McKeown, Ken, 164
Mackintosh, Charles Rennie, 103
Mackintosh, John P., 32
Maclaren, Pharic, 69-70
Maclean, Alec, 33
McLean, Bill, 31
MacLeod, Donny B., 22, 43
MacLeod of Fuinary, Lord, 96
McNaught (man who fired K.R.), 160-1
Macpherson, Archie, 70-1

Machair, 174
Mack, Jimmy, 178-9
Magnusson, Magnus, 54, 57, 181
Manson, Bill, 114, 121, 125, 127, 130, 139, 150, 157, 161
Marquis, Mary, 45, 54-5
Martin, David, 164-5
Mastermind, 55, 57, 181
Matheson, Very Rev. James, 75
Maxton, Jimmy, 11
Maxwell, Robert, 53
Maybole, 113, 116, 123
Maybole Castle, 103, 109, 131, 163
Mearns, the, 69
Meehan, Paddy, 53
Menzies, Gordon, 16, 18
Metropolitan Police, man from the, 63-5
Michael, Glen, 139
Mid-Calder station, 25

Midlothian shale industry, 17, 27
Millan, Bruce, 92
Millar, Bob, 60, 101-2
Millar, George, 28
Miller, Arthur, 173-5
Miller Road, Ayr, 164
Miller, William B., 113-4, 116-7, 122, 127, 158-60
Milne, Alasdair, 70
Milne, John, 53
Monro, Donald, 28, 36-7, 41, 43, 45, 64, 72, 95
Morris, Rev. Dr Bill, 121, 135
Morrison, Fran, 54
Munn (educational reformer), 92
Murray, Chic and Maidie, 66-7
Murray, Ruby, 140
Myers, Anne, 121
My Kind of Country, 139
Mystical Waters, 136

Nairn, Charles, 54-5, 68
National Union of Mineworkers, 31
Nationwide, 37-9, 41-2
Neil, Ron, 40-1
Nesbitt, Rab C., 70, 173
Nethy Bridge, 102
New College, Edinburgh, 74
News at Ten, 171
Niven, David, 95-6
North Berwick, 92
North Queensferry, 26
North Sea oil, 26-9
North Uist, 88, 104-6
Noyce, Dora, 76

Oakbank, 17
Observer, 169
O'Halloran, Sir Charles, 121
Old Lady Shows Her Medals, 68
Oosterhuis, Peter, 72
Open Golf Championship, 157

Pack (educational reformer), 92
Partick, parish of, 88
Pearly Gates (aka Ayr Cemetery), 131, 138
Perth, 29
Petrie, Gordon, 136
Pickles, John, 178
Piper Cherokee, doomed, 38-9, 41
Pirrie, Jim, 157
Pitlochry, 61-2
Plowden, Lady, 125-7, 129
Portobello, 17, 36
Portree, 75
Presley, Elvis, 135, 140
Prestwick, 140
Prestwick Airport, 113-4, 150
Prestwick Circuits, 113, 116
Prestwick, incident at garden gate, 102
Priestley, J.B., 64
Private Eye, 52
Pumpherston, 27
Purdy, Ernest, 11, 13, 44, 60
Purser, Philip, 170

Queen Margaret Drive, Glasgow, 33, 45-6, 56, 69, 78, 82, 90, 174
Queen Street, Edinburgh, 28, 113
Quiet Wedding, 17

Radio Aire, Leeds, 132
Radio Authority, 177
Radio Clyde, 111, 115-6, 120-5, 127, 130, 135, 139, 155, 158-9, 162, 179
Radio Forth, 135, 146
Radio Highland, 107
Radio Scotland, 63, 88, 104, 178-9, 180
Radio Times, 15, 89, 166
Radio West, Bristol, 132
Rangers Football Club, 89-90
Rantell, Kathleen, 90
Rantzen, Esther, 170
Rattigan, Terence, 124
Ravenscraig, 176
Regan, Jack, 103, 180
Reid, Very Rev. George, 75
Reid, George, 35, 164

187

Reid, Harry, 90
Reid, Jimmy, 97
Reid, Robert, 68
Reith, Lord, 56, 178
Religious Advisory Committee, BBC Scotland, 87
Reporting Scotland, 19-22, 33, 37, 40-5, 47, 71, 78, 94, 101, 103, 106, 162, 171
Ring, Professor John, 121-2
Ritchie, John, 11
Robertson, Gregor, 63
Robertson "Long Will", 88
Robertson, Sid, 169
Roller, Pat, 171
Rollo, John, 13
Ross of Marnock, Lord, 95, 153, 155
Ross, Tom, 95, 165
Roxy Theatre, Falkirk, 66-7
Roy, Christopher, 107
Roy, Kenneth: *Glasgow Herald,* 11-17; *The World of Mrs Smith,* 12-15; joins BBC Scotland, 19; *Reporting Scotland,* 19-25, 43-6; North Sea oil O.B., 27-8; coverage of elections, 31-5; *Nationwide* air race, 36-42; *Children of the Mist,* 47-50; dinner with Alastair Hetherington, 54-7; visit to Copenhagen, 58-61; suspected of murder, 63-5; introduces Edinburgh Festival O.B., 71-2; General Assembly programmes, 74-81; *Eighth Day,* 84-5; *Yes, No, Don't Know Show,* 85-7; *Crossfire,* 88-90; bugs Willie Waddell, 89-90; interviews David Niven, 95-6; interviews Hugh MacDiarmid, 96-8; leaves *Reporting Scotland,* 102-3; supernatural experience, 104-6; West Sound, 109-61; unemployed, 162-3; *Voyager,* 164; *Agenda,* 164-6; *Scotland on Sunday,* 168-76; seriously ill, 175-6; banned by

BBC, 179-80
Roy, Margaret, 17, 37, 55, 63, 92, 100, 102, 109, 121, 131, 133, 149
Roy, Stephen, 107
Royal & Ancient Golf Club, 72, 157
Royal Bank of Scotland, 114
Royal High School, Edinburgh, 35
Royal Hotel, Bonnybridge, 14-16
Royal National Theatre, 174

St Andrew Square bus station, pub at, 33
St Andrews University, 30
Savoy Park Hotel, Ayr, 110
Sayers, Dorothy L., 126-7
Scotland on Sunday, 169, 172, 176, 178-9
Scotland Today, 58
Scotsman, 90
Scott, David, 53
Scott, George, 48
Scottish Agriculture Department, 106
Scottish Assembly, 35, 46, 56-7, 107
Scottish Community Drama Association, 102, 108
Scottish Daily Express, 15, 62
Scottish Liberal Party, 78
Scottish National Party, 28, 35, 46, 55, 107
Scottish referendum, 57, 107
Scottish Television, 53, 58, 60-1, 171, 173-4
Scottish Tradition, 168
Scottish & Universal Newspapers, 110-2, 114-6, 123, 125
Selby Wright, Very Rev. Ronald, 75
Shand, Jimmy, 168-9
Sharman, Chris, 49
Shotts, 25, 168
Sinclair, George, 19-22, 25, 45, 47, 51, 54, 58, 60, 101-2, 103, 163, 165
Skelmorlie, 137
Skye, 49-50

Smiley, George, 126
Smith, Helen, 15
Smith, Iain Crichton Smith, 83
Smith, Jean Taylor, 153
Smith, Nancy Banks, 170
Smith, Ralph, 80
Smith, W. Gordon, 13
Snow, Peter, 170
Spicer, Matthew, 45, 165-6
Sproxton, Vernon, 76
Star Inn, Maybole, 103
Stark, Edi, 180
Station Hotel, Ayr, 115, 118, 121, 128, 130
Steel, Very Rev. David, 75-6
Steele, Tom, 146
Stein, Jock, 70
Stenhousemuir, 140
Stevens, Julieanne, 160
Stevenson, Celia, 151, 156-7, 161
Stevenston, 136
Stewart, Sir Andrew, 135
Stewart, Donald, 35
Stone of Destiny, 13
Stonehaven, 54
Stornoway, 35
Strathclyde Regional Council, 121
Streather, Paul, 34, 164
STUC, 53
Sunday Mail, 12, 145-6, 148, 180
Sunday Post, 36, 45, 145-6
Sunday Standard, 136, 162
Sunday Times, 26, 83, 176
Sundowners, 140
Sunset Song, 69-70
Swann, Sir Michael, 47
Swine vesicular disease, 30
System Three, 124, 126

Taggart, 70, 173
Take the High Road, 173
Taylor, C.P., 175
Taylor, Teddy, 34
Thatcher, Margaret, 156, 161, 164-5 177
Theroux, Paul, 170

Thirteen Club, Glasgow, 102
Thompson, Alan, 54
Thompson, Emma, 173
Thompson, John, 118, 121, 126, 128-9, 133, 159, 162
Thompson, Kathryn, 139
Thomson, Bob, 48
Thomson of Monifieth, Lord, 120-2
Thorburn, Iain, 73
Thurso, 50
Tillett, Richard, 158
Times, 18
Times Educational Supplement Scotland, 73
Tongue, hotel in, 49
Torrance, Bill, 169
Torrance, Very Rev. Tom, 76
Toye, John, 58-9, 60-1
Tranter, Nigel, 91
Troon, 110, 157-8
Trotter, Stuart, 99
Truesdale, Tommy, 140-1
Tully, Mark, 178, 180
Tutti Frutti, 174

Ubiquitous Chip, 66
Uddingston, 25
UK Atomic Energy Authority, 156
Usher Hall, Edinburgh, 71

Venters, Archie, 114
Vesuvius (central heating boiler), 103, 109, 131, 162
Voyager, 164

Waddell, Willie, 89-90
Walker, Ricky, 48
Warren, Alastair, 16-17
Warrilow, Bob, 94
Webster, Derek, 112, 116, 123
Webster, Ina, 148-9, 152
Webster, Sandy, 12, 145-52, 160
West Sound: formation of consortium, 109-17; first meeting with IBA, 121-3; second meeting with IBA, 125-7; negotiations with

IBA, 127-9; launch of station, 135-9; Burns Supper, 153-5; coverage of Falklands war, 156-7; JICRAR results, 157-8; KR fired, 160-1
Wheewell, Harry, 18
Whisky Galore, 67
Who's Who in Scotland, 33
Whyte, Don, 15
Wilson, Brian, 49, 89
Wilson, Gordon, 35
Wilson, Harold, 33-4, 54, 145
Wilson, Malcolm, 101
Wolfe, Willie, 28-9, 33
World of Mrs Smith, 14-15

World at One, 51
Wormit, 169
Wright, Tom, 69
Wyld, Stuart, 15
Wylie, Ron, 156
Wyllie, Robin, 132-3, 135, 138-9, 149-50, 154, 156, 159, 161

Yarwood, Mike, 95
Yes, No, Don't Know Show, 85-8, 114
Young, Alf, 165
Young, Andrew, 166
Young, Martin, 41
Younger, George, 155-6